ON THE MAKING OF GARDENS

ON THE MAKING OF
GARDENS

by Sir George Sitwell

introduction by Sir Osbert Sitwell

foreword by John Dixon Hunt

DAVID R. GODINE · Publisher · Boston

This edition published in 2003 by
DAVID R. GODINE · Publisher
Post Office Box 450
Jaffrey, New Hampshire 03452
www.godine.com

LIBRARY OF CONGRESS
CATALOGING-IN-PUBLICATION DATA

Sitwell, George Reresby, Sir, 1860–1943.
On the making of gardens / by Sir George Sitwell ;
introduction by Sir Osbert Sitwell ; foreword by
John Dixon Hunt.—1st softcover ed.
    p.   cm.
Includes bibliographical references and index.
ISBN 1–56792–238–4 (pbk. : alk. paper)
1. Landscape gardening. I. Title.
SB472.4.S58   2003
712—dc21   2003040818

frontispiece: Palazzo Giusti, Verona

FIRST SOFTCOVER EDITION
Printed in Canada

CONTENTS ᡒᡒ ᡒᡒ ᡒᡒ ᡒᡒ ᡒᡒ ᡒᡒ ᡒᡒ

ILLUSTRATIONS

I

SIR GEORGE SITWELL published his perceptive, elegant, and incisive book, *On the Making of Gardens*, in 1909. It has been reprinted four times: a limited edition from the Dropmore Press in 1949; two years later from Duckworth in London, and then Scribner's in New York, produced an edition with an introduction by Sir Osbert Sitwell and sixteen black and white photographs of Italian gardens. Finally, in 1984 Michael Russell in England buttressed Sir George's original text with a foreword by Sacheverell Sitwell, Sir Osbert's introduction of 1951, notes by Reresby Sitwell on the family gardens at Renishaw in Yorkshire, and line illustrations of garden scenes by Meriel Edmunds. These were all gathered together and issued under the title of *Hortus Sitwellianus*.

But *On the Making of Gardens* scarcely requires such elaborate support, though these efforts to keep it in the hands or on the shelves of gardenists (to use Horace Walpole's useful coinage) must be applauded. For those interested in the historical art of garden-making and intrigued by how its history is narrated, Sir George's book speaks eloquently for itself.

On the Making of Gardens is itself an historical document. Crafted, intelligent, and beautifully structured, like the great gardens of the Villa d'Este or the Villa Lante which they celebrate, Sir George Sitwell's pages are not only products of their time; but also part of an enthralling process of writing a garden history of which we are still part in the third millennium, just as the makers of Renaissance gardens were consciously part of an attempt to participate in garden traditions from classical times and renew them for their own tomorrows. It is self-evident that any work betrays, more or less overtly, the time and process of its production, but often it is what works declare covertly that is most interesting, what they assume about their larger subject that is more fascinating – in this case, the continuing relevance of Renaissance garden art to our contemporary concerns. And *On the Making of Gardens*, with its acute perspectives and observations on the art of the Italian Renaissance garden, addresses issues that our own contemporary profession of landscape architects continue to confront.

II

The biographical circumstances surrounding Sir George Sitwell's essay were explained by his sons, Sacheverell and Osbert, in their commentaries in *Hortus Sitwellianus*. Travelling in Italy after a severe illness, Sir George first began to gather the materials for his treatise. His subsequent researches and note-taking on every aspect of the subject were prodigious, yet he wears that knowledge and information lightly enough. At the same time, he took in hand the landscaping of the family's home at Renishaw – laying out the terraces, floating a lake, always more interested in its design than its horticulture.

Sir George's book was deeply rooted in its author's cultural context; Osbert Sitwell rightly describes his father's book as 'a genuine period-piece'. Yet it is not just its vague presentiment of landscapes by Alma-Tadema, sensations redolent of Maeterlinck or tonalities far-fetched from Walter Pater (all of which Osbert duly notes), nor the ubiquitous green parasol his father carried into gardens, that declare the flavor of the 1890s, which was when Sir George tells us he 'first began . . . to study old Italian gardens'.

The ethos of gardens that Sir George espoused was clearly that of the Symbolists:

> Surely it is the garden of a dream? Behind
> one like a cliff rises a palace of romance,
>   vast, august, austere; a palace over which

> in a far-off age some mighty magician has
> thrown an enchanting spell of sleep.

That he continues by (many times) invoking Wagner makes his values clear – we are in the mythological world of W. B. Yeats and the fin-de-siècle writers for the Savoy and The Yellow Book, where 'magic' and 'wizard's music' rule; where the languor of old passions that haunted Ernest Dowson is the sufficient content of art, and where the Pre-Raphaelite search for medieval materials has been refined. Here is a place where all the arts aspire to the condition of a music that Sir George claims is above all audible to garden lovers (that woman singing an 'old-world melody' in the valley below the Villa d'Este being answered by the harmonies of the perfect garden world); where the numinous rather than the phenomenal world is the privileged zone of congenial spirits. We can surely hear Carlyle's scorn of Benthamites and Dickens' satire of Gradgrind's academy in Hard Times, when Sitwell mocks the 'practical Man' who can only see firewood in the cypresses of Italian gardens or when, lifted 'over the threshold of fact', he champions the presence of the 'ideal' in some

enchanted fastness, high-walled like the Garden of Mirth in the old romance against pale Sorrow and wrinkled Care and envious

Time and all the spectres of the night. But in this unimagina-
tive age, when a necromancer who ventures even to tell a fortune
may be committed as a rogue and vagabond. . .

And hence, above all, Sitwell's emphasis upon gardens' access to our subconscious, his triumphant linking of 'the garden magic of Italy' to 'the domain of psychology,' a prime concern of artists and the intelligentsia in the 1890s and provided in the United States by William James' *Principles of Psychology* (1891) that Sitwell often cites.

But it explains, too, those quite astonishing passages of verbal description by which Sitwell communicates the visual and sensual experience of gardens; these passages are in the long tradition of *ekphrasis* (writing about the visual) that goes back at least to ancient times. But Sitwell's careful verbal descriptions of the visual and sensual art of gardens also link their author with the inter-art nostalgias of the Pre-Raphaelite and Symbolist movements that came to a head in England in the 1890s. Certainly, such ekphrastic passages are used to take the place of illustrations in *On the Making of Gardens* (as they had done in other earlier garden books before the days of photo-reproduction). But the use of words to evoke a total garden experience involving all the senses is of a piece with the new interests in psychology;

not less, it claims garden art as the supreme combination of all arts, a *Gesamtwerk* to rival Wagner's.

III

This stress upon the psychological importance
of garden experience is undeniable and valuable; it confounds and challenges those who think
design is only a matter of forms and the formal
disposition of parts or is centred wholly in horticultural expertise. Especially if we do not resist the
ebb and flow of his writing and, rather, yield ourselves to the unfamiliar eloquence of Sitwell's
prose, can we be removed once again to a view of
garden experience which draws upon its fullest
possible range. Given the barrenness of garden
thinking, now or in 1909, this plenitude is avail-
able, in part at least, only through an adequate
exposure to and knowledge of the history of garden design and, above all, of garden experience.
What sometimes may strike the modern reader
as mannered gestures to arcane references, say,
Garin le Loherain or the letters of René d'Anjou, are
better read as Sitwell's determination to access the
remotest corners of garden history to better document his claims for the fullness of garden experience. Though Osbert Sitwell seems surprised, it
is his father's 'analytic attention' to gardens that is

actually promoted and sustained, rather than disguised, by the rhetorical effects of his writing.

It is all the more surprising therefore that on one matter Sir George Sitwell remains largely silent: namely, the role of ideas or the topic of meaning in gardens, which we know was a prime constituent of Renaissance design. The reason for this is instructive and has to do with his (undeclared) historical perspective.

The narrative of *On the Making of Gardens* proceeds as follows. The creative energies of the Italian Renaissance garden were taken over and codified by the French (a nation flawed, according to Sitwell, by their dedication to 'unbending system'); André Le Nôtre 'stole the formulas of garden-making from Rome and Florence, but left the poetry behind.' This is a marvellously tendentious account: while Sitwell might be allowed his arguments against 'gaudy Versailles', the rest of Le Nôtre's work, especially the spatial excitements of Vaux Le Vicomte, of which there is nothing comparable in Italy, are wholly exceptional and quite unfairly neglected by Sitwell as he sets out this historical narrative (he somewhat redresses this imbalance later). In what he feels was a justifiable reaction to the 'monotony of the new [Le Nôtrean] style', there was a revolt against French 'formalism'; this we have come to identify with the English landscape garden, which in its own turn was more or less codified in Horace Walpole's *The History of the Modern Taste in Gardening*. Against the absurdities of this 'natural style', which 'spread like a plague over Europe', Sitwell makes some shrewd hits, some of which should set modern garden writers back on their heels ('the whole theory of the natural garden is absolutely unsound'). It is in the place of the false naturalism, the voguish picturesque of the 'natural' garden and the madly eclectic craze for follies and what the French called *fabriques*, fanciful structures of Chinese, Turkish, or other 'exotic' design, that Sitwell seeks to reactivate Italian Renaissance garden art. But in recalling its versatility and power, which he had experienced at first hand in dozens of Italian gardens and which he clearly understood so well, his determined emphasis upon its psychological effects unhappily marginalized another essential aspect of its strength – its intellectual aspects, a garden's ability to make ideas palpable. Perhaps he was afraid that to stake such a claim – which modern writers on the Italian Renaissance garden have boldly undertaken – would make Italian gardens seem too like their French successors, from which Sitwell wished (rightly) to distinguish them.

Only fleetingly does Sitwell betray that he may be neglecting a fundamental dimension of the garden style he so admires and rightly advocates. It is true that only once garden art began to be codified – by sixteenth-century Italians as well as the formulae-loving French in the seventeenth century – did certain common assumptions, habits of thinking taken for granted in the design and experience of fine gardens, get spelled out for all to read and ponder. Then we can read how gardens aspire to the condition of other fine arts by their staging of debates, competitions or *paragone* between art and nature, of how they represent, or present over again, in garden forms copies or abstractions of the larger world, and of how gardens were to be 'read' as complex statements about how owners and designers viewed their place in the locality, in the political scene and on the globe itself. All great gardens can be understood in that way, but Sitwell seems to have denied these achievements to the Italian gardens he so loved. Perhaps, because he associated – as many still do – excessive intellectuality with the French, he could not bring himself to attribute an equally rich mental world to the designers of Italian gardens.

Yet hints of these themes may be traced in Sitwell's concern with the principles of garden design; here he is more generous to Le Nôtre, though, since Le Nôtre left no theoretical or other writings behind him (any more than did Capability Brown), his 'principles' have to be extrapolated from his actual surviving designed gardens and landscapes. Yet Sitwell must have known that French principles of garden art were discussed in other treatises, like Jacques Boyceau's *Traité du Jardinage* (1638) or works by the Mollet family of gardeners; he certainly alludes to Dezallier d'Argenville's *La Théorie et la Pratique du Jardinage* (1709), where many of Le Nôtre's designs were codified. Among the principles that *On the Making of Gardens* touches upon are how a garden may 'represent the great elemental forces of Nature,' and how the surroundings of great gardens contribute to their impact. Sitwell rightly insists on the interface between gardens and adjacent zones of field or forest, for without the latter the creation of garden spaces as abstractions and elaborations of a wider and wilder nature would have far less meaning. There is every indication that Sir George knew the importance of these principles and manœuvres, even if he did not wish to bring them sufficiently to the surface to compete with the psychological effects of garden design. In the end his preferred focus is upon what he calls 'that blundering ghost-haunted miracle, the human mind' rather than the specific products of its thinking.

IV

Sitwell is sly in other ways. His text buries deft allusions to several other writings on gardening, scatters half quotations from them, or glancingly endorses aspects of Sir Henry Wotton's *Elements of Architecture*, Addison's *Spectator* essays, even perhaps Whately's *Observations on Modern Gardening*, a work celebrating the English landscape garden that other parts of *On the Making of Gardens* would suggest as a most unlikely citation! Indeed, his meditation upon associationism in the garden, upon 'the influence of scenery upon mood and character,' is a distinct link with the theoretical high point of the English landscape garden movement that he so strenuously dismisses. He is studiously silent, furthermore, on the fairly recent quarrel between Reginald Blomfield and William Robinson over architectural versus horticultural gardens, a fracas into which his own essay makes such a decisive and reasoned foray. His contribution melds a delight in the forms and sensations of gardens with a rich responsiveness to their associations and moods.

The continuing relevance, the aptness, of Sitwell's reflections on garden-making will surprise many first readers of his essay. They will almost certainly note his quite modern emphasis upon the therapeutic virtues of gardens. They will appreciate his insistence upon the fundamental weathering of gardens, perhaps linking it with their own concerns for sustainable design (design that sustains and absorbs seasonal and geomorphological change). The stress upon the 'countless aspects and manifold relations' of plants and insects in a habitat zone or 'the radiant happiness of the plants whose flowering is the expression of a desire to live. . . .' will also have a direct ecological appeal, despite a certain rotundity of writing that puts modern, diffident prose to shame.

What will be less immediately acceptable is Sitwell's determination that garden-making, for all its wealth of natural materials, is nonetheless an art; that it is an art of space which also addresses fundamental human concerns ('ancestral memories,' among other deep recesses of the psyche); that gardens, above all, have meanings, the intricacies of which give credence to the claim that gardens are the richest, the most elaborate, the most enduring and unfading of human creations and experiences.

We may note, finally, Sitwell's displeasure (reported by his son, Osbert) with the cover design that the publishers, John Murray, provided for *On the Making of Gardens*. Its 'most stilted of garden vistas' combined art deco memories of Beardsley with an abstract pattern in grey and green of pilaster, vase, citrus shrub and cypress. But it is surely a master stroke – identifying both the book's cultural provenance in the world of the 1890s and its gardenist promise, in short, its modernity. For 'Time,' as Sir George begins his essay, is indeed 'a wayward traveller...', and at the start of the twenty-first century his book returns to persuade us of the permanence, the timely quality, of gardens.

Cover of the 1909 John Murray edition of
On the Making of Gardens

BIBLIOGRAPHICAL NOTE

It is a confirmation, if one were needed, of Sir
George Sitwell's sense of the complexity and
plenitude of garden experience that an introduction to his *Essay* needs to reach out to so many
other aspects of human endeavour. Those who
want to follow up some of the references here
should consult David Ottewell, *The Edwardian Garden*
(New Haven and London, 1989), pp.5–38, for the
garden quarrels between Robinson and Blomfield;
for the general cultural context of the 1890s see my
own book, *The Pre-Raphaelite Imagination 1848–1900*
(Routledge, London, 1968). General ideas on
ekphrasis are set out by James A. W. Heffernan,
*Museum of Words: The poetics of ekphrasis from Homer to
Ashbery* (University of Chicago Press, Chicago,
1995), while some specific garden aspects of the
ekphrastic tradition are discussed in my 'Ekphrasis
of the garden', in *Interface: Image, Texte, Langages*, 5
(1994), published by the Université de Bour-
gogne in Dijon.

HORTUS CONCLUSUS
My Father and the Garden

I N THE HAPPY DAYS of the far-off first decade of the nineteen-hundreds, about the time that Princess Ena became engaged to King Alphonso, that Melba was first singing in *Madama Butterfly*, that Miss Lily Elsie was appearing in *The Merry Widow*, in short, in the golden days of good King Edward, a visitor in the spring or autumn to any of the great Italian or remarkable Sicilian gardens, especially those that were more remote, might have chanced to see a tall, distinguished-looking Englishman with a high-bridged nose, and with fair, fine hair and a slightly darker golden moustache, flourished upwards a little in the manner of the Kaiser, seated on a bench, regarding his surroundings with analytic attention. Probably he would be sitting on an air-cushion, and would be wearing a grey suit and a wide, grey hat, while beside him – for he was careful to sit in the shade – was a sun-umbrella lined with green. Not far off, within the carrying of a voice, from the thick blackness of an ilex grove would peer a ponderous figure, watchful, but with an eye for those who passed as well as for the safety of the square, varnished wicker box in his care; which each day contained a cold chicken. As he stood there he had something of an air of a night watch on a ship, and his appearance, though his skin was bronzed, or indeed copper-coloured, was as northern and national as that of the gentleman on the bench. He, meanwhile, had taken an envelope out of his pocket and was scratching on it with the stub-end of a pencil, angry or meditative remarks; crossly, how a gardener had removed the patine of lichen from a stone moulding since last he was here, or reflectively, comparing the merits where an effect of mystery was desired of broad shaded ilex with thin spired cypress, or of the various hues, textures, and sounds of varying kinds and speeds of falling water, and the sense of coolness and peace these induced. . . .

The visitors might perhaps enquire – as often they did when they got back to the hotel – who the English gentleman might be, and the nautical figure hovering so heavily in the background – and the answer would be, Sir George Reresby Sitwell and his servant, Henry Moat. For, in those years, my father was busy collecting material for the book he planned.

In 1900, he had suffered a bad nervous breakdown and had decided in consequence to give up politics. In the ensuing years he travelled much in

Italy, and of his recovery there this book was the fruit. He had already written several works of an historical nature, or illustrative of the manners of some particular period, but had issued them from his own printing press. They had not been for sale. But this new volume was to be published by Murray: and its aim was high, for I recollect him saying to me that he hoped it would rank in the future with Bacon's essay on gardens.

On the Making of Gardens certainly stands as the most complete expression in my father's writings of one facet of his personality, of one concentration of his interests – but there were hundreds of others. Though he worked so hard at all the innumerable matters on which he was engaged, the truth is that he found it difficult to finish anything. The garden at Renishaw remains – and is now likely to remain – uncompleted in its detail. And the family history at which he had worked for two decades was found after his death with still one chapter lacking.

Time seems to have been too short for him in his eighty-three years, and only this one book which follows is an idea of his conceived, attempted, and achieved – whatever may be judged of the achievement – wholly realised down to the last comma and the final full stop. Moreover, when setting himself to anything, no pain was spared, either to himself or to others – it would often have been, in result, better if it had. Thus, before beginning to write this book, he spent endless hours mastering the full intricacies of English grammar, under the tuition of Major Viburne, who appears a fitful – in every sense – shadow in the pages of my autobiography, and who knew much less about it than his pupil. In fact, my father took too much trouble. To write a sentence on the psychology of garden-making, he would read a hundred slightly obsolete technical volumes, nor would he always give his imagination room for its full sweep in the matter on which he was writing. He relied overmuch on notes – for one difference between the journalist and the writer resides in this, that the first takes notes and directly transcribes from them, while the second allows – or should allow – the subject-matter of his book to grow organically, like a plant, in the mind and on the paper. Thus, in illustration of what I mean, I once saw my father setting off from the door at Renishaw in a very old carriage, about eleven on a September night. As usually he went to bed at ten, I was surprised, and enquired what he was doing; 'Just driving down to Eckington Church to observe the effect of moonlight on the spire,' he replied with a flutter of his hand, as if conferring a favour upon the edifice; 'I want it for my chapter, *Eckington Church in the Thirteenth Century* in *Tales of My Native Village.*'

Notwithstanding, never was any book more pondered upon at every stage. For hours the author would lie on his bed wrestling with each problem, and if Henry's footstep was heard in the passage, or a hotel housemaid dared to wipe and rattle surreptitiously – a favourite trick when a writer is at work – the door handle, he would dart out of bed, clearing his mosquito net as if by magic, open the door, and look out blandly, while making at the same time a humming noise which held in it – if you listened carefully – an icy-cold, but terrible, menace. (Strangers, however, were apt to mistake this sound for one engendered by happiness, and in consequence, often received strange surprises.)

Unfortunately then, as I have said, his energies were dissipated over a field too broad for their employment. But though he was adept at taking hold of the wrong end of a thousand sticks, yet when by chance he seized the right end, his grasp of it was remarkable, because of the intellectual power and application, as well as the learning, which he brought to his task. And here, in *On the Making of Gardens*, we have a complete work containing a great deal of thought and couched in phrases often of stilted beauty, and even if the whole book from its opening 'Time is a wayward traveller' down to the closing sentence which begins 'Flying shafts of silvery splendour. . .' carries for us the haunting and mocking echo of Sir Austin Feverel's *The Pilgrim's Scrip*, even if fountains throughout are inclined to 'plash,' and the 'goat-herd' figures overmuch in a landscape not untouched by Alma-Tadema, still, it's none the worse for that, being a genuine period piece, instilled with considerable imagination, influenced by the philosophies current ten years earlier, and with, not far behind each page, those crepuscular sensations made fashionable by Maeterlinck, together with a reverberation of the august, if far-fetched, rotundities of Walter Pater. Moreover – and this is where he took the right end of the stick – the principles he enunciated in his volumes (so my gardening friends, whose judgement I trust, tell me) are invaluable in the practical design of gardens, in the counterpoint of light and shade, and the correct employment of water as a device for variation.

In short, he knew what he was talking about, having observed, noted, and practised. His knowledge of gardens, Italian in particular – was unrivalled (several later writers have had recourse to the lists obtained from him), but not, I hasten to add, of flowers, about which, paradoxically to English ideas of the present day, no man knew or

cared less, for he had early imbibed the Mediter-
ranean conception, imposed by brightness of climate, that a garden is a place of rest and peace,
and in no way intended for a display of blossoms
(for that, you had 'a flower garden' away from
the house, and hidden). Such flowers as might be
permitted, had, like all else in good taste, to be un-
obtrusive, not to call attention to themselves by
hue or scent, but to form vague pointillist masses
of colour that could never detract from the view,
and to infuse into the air a general sweetness never
to be identified. The pastel-shade sweet peas and
stocks of nineteen hundred, love-in-the-mist, a
few washed out roses, and a reed with a kind of
blue flower – these passed muster: but even they
were sacrifices to my mother's insistent demands
for scent and colour. 'Horticulturists' blossoms'
were what he most detested, and to make a personal confession, I remember that as a schoolboy
on holiday, when my father had been particularly
disagreeable, I used always to go out in the garden to tend a rhododendron that carried a purple
blossom of a peculiarly obtrusive and fiery appearance which he could see from his study window,
and which greatly offended his eye although for
some reason or other he never eradicated it. This
I did because I had been told by someone that if
you removed the dead raceme from a branch it

would flower again, and more flagrantly, the following spring.

To return to the book which follows, I remember well the initial stages of its first publication, for I had never before seen galley proofs, and my father gave them to me – I was sixteen – to read, with his corrections on them (I little knew then, how those flat paper serpents were to entangle and devour my life, as if I were Laocoön), and I used to take them into a corner of the small flat in Florence which we had rented that year, to revel in the sense of importance which this new acquaintance with the technical ways of the literary world conferred upon me . . . Not only were these the first corrected proofs I had seen, they were, alas, also the first I ever lost! . . . Eventually, after a week of utter ignominy and disgrace, they were found in a cupboard in my room where I had placed them for safe keeping. Later in the year – for publishing was then a quicker business altogether – my father's great moment arrived and the book came out – I think in September 1909. But, it is sad to recall, little more happened. One or two appreciative essays, such as were written in those more leisurely days, appeared in the weekly papers. He, and I, waited . . . but the rest was silence. Naturally he was disappointed, and blame was distributed impartially, some of it no doubt coming to me and a good deal being placed to my mother's account.

I remember, too, his remarking of the top binding of his book, which was concealed under an azure dust-cover, but displayed in bright colours the hardest and most stilted of garden vistas, that 'Murrays have managed to contradict with it every lesson I inculcate. . . .' However, he was pleased with the printing, if not with the reception. And I think, that the actual moment of the appearance of the book was most pleasant for him. He had been ill, as the reader knows, and the process of study in gardens had healed him. The publishing of his work had constituted, moreover, a declaration of independence, and an affirmation of faith. It must have brought back to him lovely sunny days spent in his own company, which he greatly enjoyed, with Henry and the luncheon-basket discreetly within call. Sometimes he took me with him, and on these occasions he was at his most amiable. There were, as well, adventures; such as that of which I heard subsequently from Henry, though I was not myself present. My father was meditating, just before the hour when the garden was to be closed, at the very bottom of the layout of Villa d'Este, between the giant cypresses. He was deep in thought, when four ancient *custodi* advanced on him from the four different quarters of the compass. Immediately, concluding the old men were brigands (for he lived always a hundred years before his time), he, as Henry put it, 'fair biffed 'em with his umbrella. You could hear 'em squawk half a mile away!'. . . But from such escapades, for which, alone of living men, he seemed qualified, he always emerged victorious and scot-free. It was enough in those days for Henry to explain that his master was an English *Signore*.

The effect, however, on my father of the lack of success of his book, was considerable. He had, he told me, hoped to earn by it, now that his world was threatened by Lloyd George's Budget, something to leave to my brother Sacheverell. This hope was disappointed. And then there was another side to it. Many of my mother's friends, violently opposed to books in general, now regarded him as a traitor who had placed himself on the wrong side of the fence. Only the Bevy, which I have described elsewhere, sent up at his approach hosannahs of faint artistic praise. Meanwhile, he set himself to problems that were more immediate and practical than the theories of garden design. He arranged to send me to an army-crammer's, from which I was seldom allowed to emerge – and when I did make a sortie, was seldom to be greeted with rapture. Then he had long been at work on an invention – a stick which would discharge vitriol at mad dogs and thus dispose of them. (There had been an epidemic of hydrophobia some twenty years before, but he had never as yet completed or patented his idea.) To this matter he now gave his mind. In addition, he made more miscellaneous notes; *Rotherham under Cromwell*, *Sheffield in the Wars of the Roses*, *Court Formalities at Constantinople*, *Marriage Chests of the Middle Ages*, *How to Preserve Fruit*, *The Correct Use of Seaweed as an Article of Diet*, *Sacheverell Pedigrees*, *My Views on Democracy*; each of these, and of a thousand other subjects, had a box devoted to it. These boxes were specially made for him, to contain half-pages of foolscap, and were fashioned of a material the colour of an aubergine, and in texture like a skin with goose flesh . . . Indeed, in every thing connected with writing, he had his own ways. His pens, as I have described elsewhere, were of a fine, scratchy variety, composed of three long nibs fitted together making them still more light and spidery in their use. For the rest, in the world of actuality, if he could not write about gardens with success, at least he could make them. He abolished small hills, created lakes, and particularly liked now to alter the levels at which full-grown trees were standing. Two old yew trees in front of the dining-room windows at Renishaw were regularly heightened and lowered; a process which I then believed could have been shown to chart, like a thermometer, the tempera-

XXXI

ture of his mood, and to which he always referred as 'pulling and dragging'. ('That oak tree needs to be pulled and dragged!') From the wooden towers constructed for the purpose in the lake and on the hill, he would measure and survey. His head throbbed with ideas, the majority of them never to be put into practice. Glass fountains, aqueducts in rubble, gigantic figures, cascades through the woods, stone boats and dragons in the water of lake and pool, blue stencilled white cows 'to give distinction to the landscape,' many of these schemes, alas, remained where they were born. But they were a fine exercise for him, and a diversion. And it must be remembered that he would be occupied, too, every day in instructing all those about him in whatever was their speciality, while at the same time he was, besides, ferociously engaged in combat over his own affairs; for, as he once rather piteously remarked to me, 'One has to think of *oneself a little*.'

TO MY MOTHER this essay is dedicated ☙ ☙ ☙

To many excellent people who take a gloomy view of life, studies of art and beauty seem to be but trifling; I must therefore urge as an excuse for this essay that the greater part of it was written during a period of broken health, when slowly recovering from the effects of over-work. Further, I would plead that a serious purpose lies behind it, namely, that of influencing the newly recovered art of garden design. The revival of garden-craft is the work of English architects, more particularly of Sedding, R. Blomfield, and F. Inigo Thomas. But still, as in the days of Fynes Moryson, the formal garden in England falls short of the great examples of the Italian Renaissance; it is seldom related as it should be to the surrounding scenery; it is often wanting in repose and nearly always in imagination. During the last few years several sumptuous volumes have appeared illustrating the old gardens of Italy, yet except for a few hints given by Mrs Wharton in her most valuable and charming book, little or nothing has been said about principles. If the world is to make great gardens again, we must both discover and apply in the changed circumstances of modern life the principles which guided the garden-makers of the Renaissance, and must be ready to learn all that science can teach us concerning the laws of artistic presentment.

Every one who has travelled in Italy appreciates the courtesy and kindness shown by Italians to strangers of all nationalities – perhaps one would not be wrong in saying more especially to Englishmen. Since I first began in the early 'nineties to study old Italian gardens I have visited more than two hundred in all parts of the country, and I cannot sufficiently express my thanks to the owners.

ON THE MAKING OF GARDENS ᏚᏚᏚ

Palazzo Giusti, Verona

Time is a wayward traveller, who sometimes rides posthaste through thick and thin, sometimes loiters on the road or falls asleep in the saddle, so that, fearing he is engulfed, we are half inclined to send with ropes and lanterns to drag him out of the deep miry ways: it is therefore not surprising if now and again the events of a century are crowded into the annals of one brief lifetime. Nowhere is this headlong rush of Time more noticeable than in the sixty years which elapsed between the publication of Bacon's essay on gardens in 1625 and that of Sir William Temple in the last year of King Charles the Second. The charm of both writers will be felt by every one, yet so different is the spirit and outlook that we seem to have passed into another world. The last wave of the great Renaissance impulse spends itself and dies in Bacon: in Temple, great events often taking their rise in a garden, we have the first suggestion of a return to nature and freedom, the first whisper of rebellion, the first breath of revolution. There is another strange difference between the two essays. Bacon, while content to work within the four-square limits which sense, moderation, and experience, have imposed, is pregnant in every sentence with suggestion, fancy, imagination: Sir William is a cold formalist intent on growing better peaches and nectarines than his neighbours, and has nothing to say which his best friend could describe as imaginative, unless it be his reference to a Dutch garden at the Cape of Good Hope, divided into four parts, each planted with the trees, flowers, and fruit peculiar to one-quarter of the world; an idea on a par with those which have inspired so many of our modern Memorials, and not, as Sir William himself must have been aware, belonging to a very high order of imagination.

In this there is something more than the different genius of the two men, something more than the baneful influence of Versailles. The world itself has changed, the day of humanism is over, new and narrower fetters are everywhere replacing the old. We have reached the age of the Classical Decadence when scholarship was sinking into pedantry, when form and correctness were more than fancy or freedom and clever technique than serious intention or high endeavour, when painting, architecture, war, poetry, love, and manners had all been reduced to rules of practice and education had come to be a knowledge of restraints. It was not permissible to admire the barbarous Gothic, nor the rugged efforts of untutored nature, nor the work of the earlier poets and masters; commerce

4

and the care of an estate were vulgar, and to think
for oneself in the realm of philosophy or religion
was not only, as at present, a misdemeanour, but
actually a crime. Thus it was that thought and freedom being denied, the fine gentlemen and radiant
ladies whom we see upon the canvases of Watteau,
Hogarth, and Longhi took to the more pardonable
vices of gambling and intrigue, to exquisite trifling
in porcelain and prints and jewels and enamels
and miniatures, or drowned the illusions of life in
a fairy world of enchanted sound. Thus it was that,
hedged in on every side by formalism, they grew
weary of the silvery plash of the fountain and the
bass murmur of the stepped cascade, of ordered
bosquet, stiff canal and sanded parterre, of groves
like green chests set upon poles, of smirking
nymphs and leering satyrs and fine vases full of
nothing. The long straight alleys seemed to them
to be insipid, the evergreen hedges to be unfeel-
ing; they hated the flower battalions which stood
on parade in platoons of pinks and regiments of
tulips and armies of asters, the stage scenery of
box and turf and trellis which could not share in
the hopes of spring or the regrets of autumn, but
was dead to all the music of the year. For in the
general decadence of the arts the garden too had
fallen upon evil days. Unbending system had been
the fault of the French, even in the time of Mon-

taigne, who notes that the Italians 'borrow an infinity of graces, not known among us, from the very irregularity of the surface'; and in the last quarter of the seventeenth century, when the sceptre of taste and fashion passed at length from proud Italy to gaudy Versailles, the evil was intensified by Le Nôtre, who stole the formulas of garden-making from Rome and Florence, but left the poetry behind.

The long-drawn-out monotony of the new style, which took no account of the genius of the place, but sought everywhere to overwhelm nature with mighty embankments and deep-dug valleys and rivers turned from their courses, with terrace heaped upon terrace, with groves of up-springing fountains and forests of well-drilled trees, was bound to provoke a reaction. But the revolution which followed is not an isolated phenomenon: with the baroque in architecture, the Chinese taste in decoration, the freer forms of musical composition, the Romantic movement in painting and literature, it is part of a world's revolt against a formalism which had become intolerable.[1] At first the English garden, the garden of nature and sentiment which Addison and Rousseau describe, must have appeared by contrast as refreshing as in these days of lawns and shrubberies a walled enclosure is to us. In the parks attached to the great houses, where oval lakes and square islands were not unknown, there was room for the new landscape art, whose great achievement has been the management of water and the grouping of trees. But as under Louis XIV the garden had encroached upon the park, so now the park swept over the garden, bringing the 'one unending undulating sweep' of the bare English lawn up to the very windows of the house. With the Peace of 1762 the new fashion spread like a plague over Europe, destroying everywhere the historic and harmonious setting of hall and palace and castle, scenes which the care and love of by-gone centuries had hallowed, which should have been left to us to link one generation with another. In its train came follies worse than those which provoked the satire of Addison. The garden was deprived first of its boundaries and then of its flowers; sham rivers, dead trees, and broken bridges were planted in appropriate positions, while over the countryside in the neighbourhood of the great houses there broke out a dreadful eruption of Gothic temples and Anglo-Saxon keeps, Corinthian arches and Druid amphitheatres, of classic urns, Chinese pagodas and Egyptian pyramids, all with inscriptions in Greek or black-letter appealing to the eye of taste and to the tear of sensibility.

Modern writers who wish to make the best of

both gardening worlds endeavour to excuse these aberrations as excesses for which the style itself must not be held responsible, but though much may be said for the simple garden, the whole theory of the natural garden is absolutely unsound. If the house requires a platform as a statue requires a pedestal, if the bold projections and broad shadows of terrace and stairway are peculiarly valuable in the foreground, if water in a small volume is ridiculous or squalid unless set off by formal masonry, if standing pools double by reflection the beauty of flowers and trees, if the contrast of vegetation and stonework is dear to the heart of every artist, why are we to sacrifice all these advantages to a sentiment which has not even the merit of being sincere? 'You will observe,' says the landscapist, introducing us to his ideal pleasure ground, 'that here there is nothing regular, nothing artificial, no straight lines or pleached hedges or tonsured trees; only a loving and reverent study of beautiful Nature's methods and a patient attempt to reproduce her pictures: the idea is that we are in a natural glade of the forest.' Quite so, we venture to remark, but what about the mown grass and the rather undecided gravel path and the scentless roses and the rich and startling masses of horticulturists' flowers and the unhappy blotches of subtropical foliage? 'We must assume', he replies, 'that this is a kind of grass that doesn't grow and that the gravel path is an unfortunate accident.' Very well, we say again, anxious to enter into the spirit of the thing, but what about the house; is that an unfortunate accident too? It is indeed upon this point that the theory of the landscape garden goes to total shipwreck. You can't hope to persuade us that Nature built the house: why insult our understanding by pretending that Nature made the garden? The utmost extreme to which artificiality can go is the mock-natural. If this be defended on the ground that the garden is a land of illusion in which any fraud is permissible, we are bound to point out that it is a deception which fails to deceive; if on the other hand we are asked to accept it as a frank convention, what is to be thought of all this high-flown sentiment about the graceful touch of Nature? No mastery over form can save from failure a work of art animated by a faulty or defective idea. Now Hegel has pointed out in his Æsthetics that the affectation of want of purpose and contrivance, the presence of disorder, of natural primeval solitude in an artificial scene which has been deliberately planned for human enjoyment and for social intercourse, is one of those primary discords which no ingenuity can soften or conceal, for the jarring note will be heard above all the music of the landscape. In such a scene civilised man is out of place, and even the landscape gardener who contrived it must follow the example of the ancient Britons and put on a suit of woad, if he wishes to be in harmony with the surroundings. Yet another discord in the motive is that between the house and the woodland lawn upon which it has apparently dropped from the skies: the house is at war with the landscape and the landscape with the house, each has a different tale to tell, and no natural beauty of flower or tree can relieve us from the shock of contradiction and the pain of incongruity. Curving paths cannot be right, for the Chinese themselves, with whom the landscape style began, make their paths straight, arguing that they must be due either to design or to repeated passage, that no sober man will deliberately propose to reach his destination by a series of curves, and even if the inhabitants of a house or hamlet were to get drunk in company, that it is hardly possible they should all describe precisely the same reel of intoxication. Flower-beds in stars or moons or rounded figures cannot be right: they are simply unquiet and, as Ruskin points out, straight lines are the best foil to the grace of natural curves in plant and flower. It cannot be right to endeavour to realise in a garden the compositions of the great masters of painting, for that is to sacrifice general beauty to a few selected points of view, and how is one to compose a picture with changing materials when the foreground is wandering into the middle distance, the figures and the cattle are moving on, the saplings are burgeoning into a grove? It cannot be right to crowd together in a few acres all the mood – compelling aspects of nature, the gay, the tranquil, the romantic, the picturesque, the melancholy, the tragic, the terrible, the sublime; or to fill the park with abbeys and hermitages, Greek temples and Gothic castles, which are both incongruous with each other and through meanness of scale and poverty of material do not deceive but only offend. That indeed is the final outcome of the landscape garden: it appeals to many emotions but touches only one, a peculiar kind of heart-sinking which one remembers to have experienced before upon entering some Chippendale-Gothic mansion belonging to the same period of art.

Is it not time that the world should abandon these follies of the Decadence, should turn again for inspiration to the 'high walled gardens green and old' of a happier time; that it should listen at last to the prayer of the eighteenth-century poet:

Again the moss-grown terraces to raise
And spread the labyrinth's perplexing maze,

*Cascade and
Hydraulic Organ,
Villa d'Este, Tivoli*

Replace in even lines the ductile yew
And plant again the ancient avenue;

that it should turn its back on Kent, Capability
Brown, and Horace Walpole, and should seek
to learn the principles of garden design from
Alberti, Michelozzo, Bramante, Vignola, Raphael,
Michelangelo?

For more than two centuries the gardens of the
Italian Renaissance lay under a cloud, exciting, it
would seem, little but contempt and disgust in all
who viewed them. Misson [1] writes in 1688 that
in magnificence the gardens of France so far surpass those of Italy, that the best way to save the
credit of Frascati and Pratolino is to pass over in
silence all the pretty wonders that were once so
highly extolled; and speaks with something like
contempt of Villa d'Este, which only cost three
million francs to build, while the very lead of
the canals at Versailles was worth all Tivoli put
together. A writer in the *Landscape Annual* for 1831
remarks of Villa d'Este that though delightfully
situated, it is deformed by the bad taste in which
the grounds about it are disposed. An English
traveller, twenty years later, brings a still more
sweeping indictment against the gardens of Frascati: they want character and expression, belong
to the dark ages of art; with so profuse an expen-

[1] *Numerals in brackets refer to 'References in the Text' on page 124.*

diture it is wonderful that so little invention has been displayed and that so little beauty has been the result.[2]

Let us turn our steps to Italy, and see how far such strictures are justified. These old Italian gardens, with their air of neglect, desolation, and solitude, in spite of the melancholy of the weed-grown alleys, the weary dropping of the fern-fringed fountains, the fluteless Pans and headless nymphs and armless Apollos, have a beauty which is indescribable, producing upon the mind an impression which it is difficult to analyse, to which no words can do justice. In all the world there is no place so full of poetry as that Villa d'Este which formalist and naturalist united to decry. Driving past the little Temple of Vesta, high above the seething cauldron of the Anio, one is admitted through vaulted corridors and deserted chambers where faded frescoes moulder on the wall to a stairway overhanging the garden. And the garden that lies in the abyss below, terrace after terrace looking out upon the wooded mountain flank and far mysterious plain – surely Time has forgotten these giant cypresses which lift from the gulf dark pinnacles of night, great rugged, gloomy-verdured spires; surely it is the garden of a dream? Behind one like a cliff rises a palace of romance, vast, august, austere; a palace over which in a far-off age some mighty magician has thrown an enchanting spell of sleep. Sleep and forgetfulness brood over the garden, and everywhere from sombre alley and moss-grown stair there rises a faint sweet fragrance of decay. In the valley below a woman's voice is singing an old-world melody, sad and pure and strange as the Spinning-song of Wagner; a tune which tells of a prisoned soul and the longing to be free. And still one may listen to the magic of the wizard's music, for the muffled thunder of the great cascade dominates the whole garden, and above it, blended like the rolling of the spheres into one deep melodious thrill, are the varying notes of murmuring, mourning, whispering, rioting, rejoicing water.

On the left, the garden looks down upon gray-green olives shot with silver in the sunlight, and upon a vine-clad pergola which clings like a spider's web to undulating slope and dell. Deep drifts of withered leaves have gathered on the stairways, the fountain basins are overgrown with maidenhair or choked with water-weeds, the empty niches draped with velvety moss or tapestried creepers. Descending by weed-grown stair and crumbling balustrade, one reaches a gloomy alley where a hundred fountains gush into a trough beneath a line of mouldering reliefs. At the further end of the terrace, falling in great cascades like the folds of a Naiad's robe or the flash of a silver sword, the river leaps into the garden, to four great pools of troubled water, a jewelled belt which quivers in the sunlight with a mysterious, an amazing blue. Such is the garden in the sober daylight, but what it may be in the summer nights, when the breath of the ivy comes and goes in waves of drowsy perfume, and great white moths are fluttering about the fountains, and in the ilex arbours and gloomy alcoves there are strange mutterings, and deep-drawn sighs, and whispering voices, and flashes of ghostly white, I do not dare to say.

The Duke of Lante's garden is of another character, a place not of grandeur or tragedy but of enchanting loveliness, a paradise of gleaming water, gay flowers, and golden light. The long, straight, dusty road from Viterbo leads at length by a bridge across a deep ravine to a gap in the town walls of Bagnaia, 'twixt Gothic castle and Barocco church, then turning at a right angle in the piazza one sees in front the great Renaissance gateway which opens into the garden. But it is better, if permission may be obtained, to enter the park, and striking upward by green lawns and ilex groves to follow from its source the tiny streamlet upon which pool, cascade, and water-temple are threaded like pearls upon a string. Dropping from a ferny grotto between two pillared *loggias*, this rivulet rises again in an elaborate fountain surrounded by mossy benches set in the alcoves of a low box hedge. Four giant plane trees lift a canopy against the sun, and tall stone columns rising from a balustraded wall warn off the intruding woodland. Thence, running underground, it emerges unexpectedly in the centre of a broad flight of steps between the claws of a gigantic crab – Cardinal Gambara's cognisance – and races down a long scalloped trough, rippling and writhing like a huge snake over the carved shells which bar its passage. From this it drops over the edge of a small basin between two colossal river-gods into a pool below. The fall to the next level gives us a half-recessed *temple d'eau*, with innumerable jets and runlets pouring from basin to basin; and here, flanked by stately plane trees and by the two pavilions which make up the *casino*, is a grass-plot commanding the loveliest view of the garden. Before us lies a square enclosure jutting out into the vale below, with high green hedges, sweet *broderies* of box bordered by flowers, and in the midst a broad water-garden leading by balustraded crossways to an island fountain which rises like a mount to four great figures of sombre-tinted stone. Water gushes from the points of the star which the naked athletes uplift, from the mouths of the lions by their side, from the masks on the balustrade, from the tiny galleys in which vagrant cupids are afloat upon the pools. It is a colour harmony of cool refreshing green and brighter flowers, of darkest bronze, blue pools, and golden light. Much there is of mystery in the garden, of subtle magic, of strange, elusive charm which must be felt but cannot wholly be understood. Much, no doubt, depends upon the setting, upon the ancient ilexes and wild mountain flank, the mighty hedge of green at the further end with its great pillared gateway and the dark walls and orange-lichened roofs of the houses and tower irregularly grouped behind it; upon the quiet background, the opal hues of green, violet, and grey in the softly modelled plain, and shadowy outlines of the distant hills. But the soul of the garden is in the blue pools which, by some strange wizardry of the artist, to stair and terrace and window throw back the undimmed azure of the Italian sky.

The Giusti garden at Verona strikes yet another chord, a motive not of sweet or sombre or tragic, but of intensely solemn loveliness. Driving across the bridge along a dull and dusty street, the carriage stops at a stuccoed house with painted architecture, not much better than the rest. But when the heavy entrance doors are swung back, an enchanted vista holds the traveller spell-bound – the deep, refreshing green of an avenue of cypresses half a millennium old,[2] leading to a precipice crowned by the foliage of a higher garden. For pure sensation there is nothing in Italy equal to this first glimpse through the Giusti gateway. It is but the nature of a single tree, yet presented with such mastery that the traveller is inclined to doubt the evidence of his eyes. 'Can it be true,' he asks himself, 'can anything in the world be so beautiful?' The little entrance court is bounded by high battlemented walls, and in the centre tall piers set with obelisks frame in the view; a gravel walk slopes upward in a hollow curve between the trees, until, the ascent becoming too abrupt, it breaks into three flights of steps, diminished in breadth in order to increase the effect of distance: these lead to a dark cavernous recess in the face of a rocky precipice, planted above with such a wild riot of jagged cypresses as might serve for a painted scene of a witches' sabbath. Toiling upwards through a tower built against the face of the cliff one reaches terrace walks above, and a two-storied garden-house, where summer days may be spent high above the toil and turmoil of the town. Here, from a projecting balcony, one may look down upon the venerable trees, upon the green parterres with their fountains and statues sloping upwards to the base of the rock, and upon such a maze of ribbed tiling and crooked streets as may be seen from many a northern minster tower. Far away in the blue Lombardic plain lie the domes and meres of Mantua; the town stretches towards them in a sea of ruddy-brown roofs breaking round ancient towers and spires; on the right are the mountains of the Tyrol, on the left through garden and vineyard and mulberry-grove runs the faint blue line of the Adige. Yet it is not to distant city or purple mountain or bright-flowing river that memory returns, but to the narrow alley, girt in by sheer precipices of green, which leads by cave and turret and winding stair to the secret garden upon the hill. This little pathway, where twenty generations have come and gone under the shadow of cypresses tall as the towers of Verona and older than the oldest palaces, has a grave and haunting beauty which hardly seems to belong to the existing order of things: it might have led to the place of an oracle, to the garden of Plato, the tomb of Dante, the cavern where sleeps the Venus of the ancient world.

These are the three great gardens of Italy, for the charm of Caprarola lies only in the Canephoræ – in the giant guard of sylvan divinities, playing, quarreling, laughing the long centuries away, which rise from the wall of the topmost terrace against the blue distance of an immeasurable amphitheatre walled in by far-off hills. Isola Bella, again, is a thing by itself, not a garden, but a mirage in a lake of dreams; a great galleon with flower-laden terraces and fantastic pinnacles which has anchored here against a background of purple mountains on its return to the realm of rococo. For other work of the first rank we must turn to smaller schemes or to parts of gardens, to the balustraded pool at Frascati, the water-theatre of the Villa Aldobrandini, the lemon grove of the Isolotto at Florence. Of these the last is probably known to every one who has visited Italy. It is an oval lake encompassed by a broad pathway in the shadow of a mighty wall of ilex. Marble seats are set under the green canopy, and quaint baroque fountains from curving shells and gullets of sea-monsters drop tiny rills into the lake, where merman and sea-nymph on water-horses are wildly urging their steeds towards the shore. In the centre of the island a gigantic basin of stone supports three seated figures bracketed against the pedestal of John of Bologna's splendid statue of Oceanus. But the glory of the Isolotto is in its balustrade, where instead of pilasters we have sweeping curves cut away to admit great red garden-vases, which with their burden of green and gold are doubled upon the water film, far above the clouds that are sailing through the blue gulf below.

Villa Torlonia at Frascati is not like Villa d'Este, where the great heart of the Anio throbs through the garden and every grove and thicket and alley is filled with a tumult of sobbing sound. It is a place of mysterious silence, of low-weeping fountains and muffled footfalls; a garden of sleep. The gates are on a lower level, and athwart the rose-tangled slope to the left the architect has thrown five great slanting staircases of stone, broad enough and splendid enough to carry an army of guests to the plateau above. But this is now a solitude, a mournful ilex *bosco* with cross walks and mossy fountains shaped like the baluster of some great sundial. From the central stairway, not far from the house, a broader opening in the woodland leads to a lawn and pool below the great cascade. In front is a long cliff crowned with ilex forest and faced with a frontispiece of moss-grown arches and bubbling fountains. The main fall drops from a balcony between two tall umbrageous ilexes which rise on either hand like the horns of an Addisonian periwig; from basin to basin it drops in a silver fringe, held in by low serpentine walls that curve and re-curve like the arches of a bridge or the edges of a shell. Through vaults on either hand, long winding stairways follow the curves, the masonry is choked with ferns, the steps with weeds, and riotous water-plants crowd upon the ledges or thrust green juicy stems through the scum which has gathered in the corners of the pools. At the top, in a small irregular clearing walled by wild ilex wood and wilder tangle of flowering shrubs, is a balustraded basin in the form of a great *quatrefoil*. Gold-red fish gleam in the sea-green water, which reflects soft foliage and lichened stone and patches of pearly light; in the centre a huge cylinder of moss supports the silvery feathers of a fountain; it is an enchanted pool in a fairy woodland. But the traveller who has wandered here alone on a drowsy afternoon does not linger to listen to the trickle of the fountain and the murmuring of the bees. From below the threshold of the mind a strange sense of hidden danger oppresses him, an instinct neither to be reasoned with nor to be understood. Can there be brigands yet in the forest heights, or is the place haunted by shades of the soldiers who once fell in battle about the pool? He waits and wrestles with his folly, then sadly descending the slippery stairways leaves cooling fount and shaded alley for the torrid sunshine of the outer world.

It is death to sleep in the garden.

For smaller schemes, showing how a great effect may be produced within a narrow compass, the architect will turn to the Cicogna garden at

Varese, Villa Gamberaia near Florence; perhaps one should add Villa Bernardini in the neighbourhood of Lucca. Other gardens there are which seem to have worked out the ultimate possibilities of some particular problem. At Bogliaco, on Lake Garda, a road intervenes between the hillside pleasure-ground and the palace, which is by the shore. On either flank of the house is a little terrace and bridge across the road, walled on the outside to screen the view, and from these bridges walks backed by tall yew hedges sweep round in a semi-circle to the central ascent, with its double stair-ways adorned with arcading and statuary.[3] The public highway, losing its character, has become a private approach. At Cadenabbia, a footpath along the shore cuts off Villa Carlotti from the lake. Here the *casino* is on a higher level, balustraded stair-ways lead down to a circular garden with a grace-ful baroque fountain, and hedges twenty-five feet high curving forward in plan cover the path, con-ceal the flat uninteresting water-edge, and concen-trate the view. At Castello d'Urio on Como, a late sixteenth-century garden with many statues, a public road offers the same difficulty, which is overcome by a stepped approach and bridge lead-ing to a gate of hammered iron. Villa Borghese at Frascati has a garden at two levels, a great semi-circular court disengaging the house and giving light and air to the lower rooms. Castello near Florence and Villa Imperiale at Genoa deal with the difficulties of a sloping site, where the straight walks are on a gentle and easy decline and the terraces lean to the house. Castelazzo, a few miles from Milan, Villas Gori and Sergardi at Siena, Villa Reale near Lucca, Villa Garzoni at Collodi, and the garden of the Castelnuovo Institute at Palermo, illustrate the charm of rustic theatres; Villas Bernardini, Senese, Mansi, Reale, all in the Lucca neighbourhood, the beauty of balustraded pools; the Colonna garden at Rome, Villa Cicogna at Varese, Villa Pliniana on Lake Como, the summer delights of a central cascade; Villas Borghese and Mondragone at Frascati, the advantage, even in the country, of a retired or secret garden on the level of the first floor, opening out of study or saloon.

Of the town gardens first introduced by Epicurus at Athens, Italy furnishes many examples. The Colonna palace at Rome is connected by four graceful bridges with its terraced retreat across the roadway, where fountain and cascade, box, ilex, and cypress cover the giant cornices of the Baths of Constantine. At the Castle of Ferrara, the old terrace-garden is still in existence, and at Mantua there is a *giardino pensile*, supported by five great tunnels of brick; which, however, loses its effect for want of outlook. At Vicenza the garden attached to the Palazzo Bonin slopes upwards at the further end and to the right, where a balustraded terrace over some outhouses leads to a projecting wing occupied by a great saloon. At Genoa there are several gardens raised above the level of the street, as at the Palazzo Durazzo Pallavinci. At Lucca, the fortress-palace of the Guinigi has its garden of flower-beds and ilexes upon the summit of the tower. But the great majority of these palace gardens lie on the level of the street, and there are few of the older cities which will not yield to the passing traveller some glimpse of fairyland, some vista of fern-draped niche or mossy fountain, of Neptune with his trident or Hercules with his club, or of a green *cortile* seen through the rolling curves and rusty scroll-work of a rococo gateway.[4] He is toiling through the hot, dusty street of Verona on a torrid day in June, when fierce sunshine beats back from wall and pavement and roadway; the cool breath of the mountains whispers in his ear, and there through the portal of the Canossa palace lies the foaming river twenty feet below; beyond it blue vineyard slopes and a chain of snowy peaks: a little terrace, some seventy yards long, overhangs the water, which curves outward to the rose-red towers of the embattled bridge, the brown roofs and fortress walls of the ancient city. Or, on an April morning when the

Palazzo Marcello Durazzo, Genoa

call of Spring is in the air, he is passing along the
Via S Marco at Vicenza, in the centre, for all that
may be imagined, of a spider's web of tiresome
streets, and there through the open doorway of
the Quirini palace is the country – swift-flowing
brooks and a sweet level of meadowland yellow
with buttercups. An avenue of hornbeam on either
hand walls out the town, and in the centre a formal approach, a quarter of a mile long,[5] bordered
by statues, vases, and green pyramids of lignum vitæ,
leads to a moated mound crowned by a classic
temple. When he has crossed at length the broad,
clear water, and is mounting towards the great
stone pines which cast their shadow over the
building, a fresh surprise awaits him, for, ringing
almost three-quarters of the horizon, there rises
before his eyes a tremendous amphitheatre of
mountains.

Nowhere are these garden vistas more delightful and more varied than at Bergamo, where one
cortile looks out upon a long line of giant ramparts
curtained with creepers, and bright with red and
white valerian and golden snapdragon; another
upon a wooded hillside and an enfilade of mountain peaks; another upon a green ocean that
stretches as far as the eye can reach, a vast interminable level of mulberry-wooded plain. And
there is a peculiar fascination in the upward views

through grate and pillared court and further arch-
way deep in shadow, across sunny gardens backed
by green foliage of bay or laurel, to the huge grey
bastions crowned by chestnut trees, the random
tiers of tall red-roofed houses, the towers, belfries
and cupolas of the ancient *città* on the hill. These
long vistas which pierce a succession of buildings
and enclosures seem to appeal to the sentiment of
power, and there is some mysterious charm in the
alteration of light and shadow, the contrast of formal masonry and random creepers, in the effect
of gloom with light beyond, the seclusion of a
secret garden far withdrawn from the dust and
traffic of the street. How much do the wayfarer
and the poorer town-dweller owe to these delightful confidences, to the mountain breeze which
cools the air, the touch of romance which relieves
the monotony of city life, and like a rose in winter glows with the promise of a brighter world!

For the dwellers in other cities where nature
is shyer and more retiring, that kindly magician
the scene-painter has called lake, mountain, and
river into the street. Placed behind a pillared
screen, with a fountain or strip of garden in the
foreground, these landscapes are strangely deceit-
ful. Beyond the *cortile* of the Palazzo Raimondi at
Cremona one sees through a tall arch garlanded
with twisted stems and smothered with trailing

leafage of wisteria and ivy, a distant view of Alpine
lake and heights, perhaps of the mountain home
from which the family came. Beyond the strip of
garden, a boat lies on the beach of the lake, which
reflects like a sheet of glass the towers and houses
of a little town set in the shadow of a mighty cliff.
This scene is painted upon a wall shaped to the
profile of the hills. The decorative scheme of the
Palazzo Costa[6] at Piacenza, though more elaborate, is hardly so successful. A marble balustrade
adorned with statues and urns divides the court
from the garden, beyond which is a wall serrated
to a mountain outline: but here Time, with his
greys and greens and umbers, has followed on the
heels of the landscape-painter, and bridge and terrace, woodland and precipice are mouldering away.

But it is in Brescia, above all places, that the
painted vista reigns, for here a southern imagination has run riot, and the stranger may make his
choice of time and place and season, of Goth or
Roman, of spring or autumn, of tropic palms or
Arctic snows. Here beyond the palace courts are
great pointed vaults and ruined castle halls, Renaissance loggias, wild rococo fantasies of pillared
porticoes, of crumbling theatres, of interminable
arcades. Here are lake scenes with vast planes of
stubborn rock lifting themselves into the sky, tiny
hamlets clustering round a church tower upon

the mountain side, bright palaces gleaming on the water edge, while all the landscape seems to swoon in a white haze of heat. Here on the bosom of a mystic river, leading from nowhere to nowhere, a slow boatman with averted face is ever seeking to raise an unprofitable sail; and here are dreams of the old Roman world before the fall which make one tremble at the sound of a church bell, for by stream or cataract the shepherd is piping to his flock, and under the shadow of the great stone pines shine out the marble statues and temples of the Gods.

Of the principles which guided the great Renaissance garden-makers it is not so easy to speak, for it was in poetry, in imagination that they reigned supreme, and inspiration is a breath of the muses which may not be brought within the rules of art. Their first thought was for the æsthetic impression upon the individual, for sentiment and emotion, for intellectual suggestion, for chords struck upon those vague, nebulous, spectral feelings which are ever trembling upon the threshold of consciousness. To them the garden seemed to be only half the problem, the other half was that blundering ghost-haunted miracle, the human mind. Thus they learnt the value of striking contrast; of sudden and thrilling surprise; of close confinement as a prelude to boundless free-

dom; of scorching sun as a prelude to welcome
shade or cooling river; of monotony, even of ugliness, set for a foil to enchanting beauty, as a discord is used in music, as the lowered tone of a
landscape brings out the fires of sunset or the
primrose light of dawn, as a dwarfish figure on a
Greek sarcophagus gives grandeur to a frieze of
fighting heroes. Their work, like that of all great
artists, is full of mystery, of haunting beauty, of
magic which all must feel but few can understand.
Take, for example, the treatment of water. The
Italian mastery over the 'water-art' has been dealt
with by a score of writers, who have failed to
notice that a higher poetry may be found in that
element than the beauty of form and sound, than
the shifting curves of a fountain or the deep-toned
music of a great cascade. There is the poetry of
colour. Surely some one of these writers must
have noticed the blue of the Vatican fountain,[7] the
greenish tint of the basin at Caprarola, the mysterious reflections of the water-garden at Lante
which strangely and beyond experience mirrors
the sky. But, fresh it may be from the lovely
colouring of Como and Maggiore, or from the
blue-crystal strand of Garda, where the sunlight
is ever dancing in a magic web over the pebbles,
they have attributed these effects to any cause but
the right one; to happy chance, to the depth or

33

purity of the water, the clearness of the atmosphere, the glowing radiance of the southern sun. At the Villa Borghese at Frascati a little basin some twelve feet across gives away the secret; the clipped ilex which surrounds it has been planned to cut off lateral reflections, admitting only bright sunshine from above; the beauty is due not to accident but to design. These great Italians had learnt to play with water as a sultan with his jewels, as Turner played with light; prisoning the blue of the sea in a tiny pool, the green of the chrysoprase in a fountain basin, the iris of the rainbow in a crystal spray; making it glow like a ruby with blood-red marbles, or quiver in the sunshine with the blue light of Capri, or throw back as from a mirror the deeper azure of the Italian sky.

Nowhere, except in Italy, can one learn the magnificence of the raised approach. The upward slope at the Marchese Ferrasan's at Savona, bordered by orange trees in great red vases, must be twenty feet above the garden where it meets the marble terrace, opposite the centre of the house. At Loano, midway between Alassio and Savona, is a still finer approach, an arched bridge great as a Roman aqueduct, connected with what is apparently a small castle. Perhaps the grandest of all is that which leads to the modern Villa Pallavicini at Pegli, where huge retaining-walls of stone a quarter of a mile long and in places not less than sixty feet high lift up a roadway bordered with flowers and shaded by an ilex avenue. For the greater part of its course this road points at a corner of the *casino*, but presently curves away to the left in order to strike the nearer end of the garden terrace. At the Villa Albertini at Lecco on Lake Como, the sloping stairway of grass and stone has a drop of from six to ten feet on either hand; a difference in level of even a foot is of value, as may be noticed in the Abbondi garden at Riva.

The Italian love of looking down from a height upon a great parterre of flowers finds expression in the Roman gardens of the Vatican, Villa Medici, and Villa Pamphili. Another favourite motive in Italian gardens is coolness in the summer heat, and few of the larger houses are without a grotto adorned with fountain and marble floor and encrusted with sea-shells or fantastic pebble-work. Evelyn speaks of the rooms under the great fountain in the Pitti Palace, not perhaps so delightful a retreat as that in the bridge at Blenheim; and describes the water alley at Pratolino, from the sides of which slender streams rose in the air, making a perfect vault and falling interchangeably into each other's channels, so that a horseman might ride from one end to the other without a single drop being spilt upon him. The Villa Pliniana near Como is built in the shade of a wooded cliff upon a foundation of earth and stones flung down from above, and through the central loggia a foaming cascade leaps to the lake, filling the whole house with the refreshment of its coolness and the tumult of its sound. At the Villa di Papa Giulio one may dine in a watery saloon, surrounded by running streams and bubbling fountains. The court of the papal Palace at Viterbo hangs in mid-air over a mighty arch of stone; on either side long benches are set against an open arcade of interlaced arches, and to the central fountain water rises from below through a great octagonal pillar which runs into the vault. It was built by the wizard Pope, John XXI, who in 1277 was crushed to death in an adjoining chamber by diabolic agency, for suddenly as he laughed in pride at the splendour of his work the avenging roof fell in ruin upon his head. To one of the grottoes of the Aldobrandini garden at Frascati secret conduits used to bring in a current of air strong enough to keep a copper ball dancing a yard above the pavement; and here again the whole scheme of house and garden is planned for summer shade and coolness. At the back, a wooded hill almost overhanging the palace has been cut away in a great semicircle to form a rustic theatre of fountains, so that sitting in the great saloon one may

Loggia Papale, Viterbo

see the frigid stream from Monte Algido racing down in cascade and cataract and long sloping aqueduct to two tall pillars of stone, which it mounts in a spiral curve, then falls with the sound of a cannonade upon an heroic figure of Atlas tottering under the weight of a deluged world. Or, turning one's chair, one may look out over the vast stretches of the Campagna, the most impressive plain in Europe, and feel on one's cheek the gentle breeze which plays upon the hillside, blowing from the distant sea.

Even the detail of Italian garden architecture is well worth the study of the designer. For screens or niches to terminate a terrace he will turn to the Imperiali and other gardens at Genoa rather than to Tivoli or Frascati. From many of the villas about Rome, Florence, and the Lakes, he will learn to frame in his views and close his vistas with triumphal arches or grand pillared frontispieces which fill the eye; to get on a scale with his stairways, making the risers only of stone, the treads of pebble or gravel or beaten earth;[8] to obtain a rough or rustic surface for niches and great wall-fountains by stones or pebbles embedded in mortar;[9] to make his piers of stately height and his iron gates plain and bold, without ornament except for the curved outline at the top. How inferior are the gateposts at Montacute at Drayton, even at Hampton Court, to those at Frascati or Albano, or the splendid piers in the Botanic Garden at Palermo! He will learn to relieve plots of turf with statues, and masses of reflected light upon the surface of a pool with mermen on water-horses, or little flower-laden galleys, or cupids astride on plunging dolphins. Villa Arsen at Hyères, the Grand Hotel at Varese, Villa Crivelli at Inverigo will teach him the grace and freedom of wide rococo stairways with curving fronts; Castelazzo, Albissola near Savona, and not a few of the Florentine and Roman gardens, the warmth and cheerfulness of great lemon-pots[10] in a box parterre under the windows of the house. Villa Medici at Rome will show him the importance of putting sculptured reliefs upon piers and pedestals and balustrade rests. At Val San Zibio near Battaglia, he will observe the superiority of box hedges to yew, both for their sweetness and their fresher green; at Villa Bernardini in the neighbourhood of Lucca, the grandeur of evergreen walls thirty feet high which shut out the lowlands and frame in the mountain vistas.

Villa Medici, Rome

The Italian feeling for sensation has often been spoken of. Perhaps the best example of this is furnished by another villa at Frascati, the great sixteenth-century pleasure-house of Mondragone which was built and altered and added to by a succession of popes and cardinals.

From the gate on the Monte Porzio road, a long dark avenue of cypress points at the palace, as a cannon at a star, but the easier and more usual approach is to the right between sweet box hedges shaded by forest trees. Higher up is an ilex avenue, under which the ground is bright in spring with the rose and mauve of the wild anemone and bolder pink of the cyclamen: groves of olive cut off the distant views, and near the house the avenue is doubled and trebled with older, darker, gnarlier trees. The carriage stops between a huge walled recess in the hillside drowned in a cataract of ivy and a plain stuccoed palace-front with simple pillared entrance and square window-frames of stone. Passing through the great quadrangle, remarkable only for scale and austerity, except for a small recessed front at the further end where the Borghese dragons writhe in stone between the pilasters, one enters a gloomy hall and beyond it a small square chamber with painted ceiling and stuccoed figures, a chamber which might be the ante-room to some splendid gallery or imposing saloon, but cannot have been designed as the terminus of so stately an approach. However, there is nothing beyond but a little iron balcony, and after so much gloom and confinement as you step out upon it the boundless view takes your breath away.

Far below the level of the palace windows there opens an immeasurable plain, stretching out mile after mile, league after league, day's journey beyond day's journey, until at last the purple distance melts at the world's edge into a silvery gleam of sea. This immensity of level space is not monotonous, as a meaner plain might be, for it is various in all its parts, embracing rich pasture-lands of feathery grasses and stony desolate stretches, tall pine forests and grave-green marshes, low cliffs and wandering streams; and it is responsive to every mood of the passing seasons or of the flying hours, from the first flush of dawn, when the trailing mist-wreaths rise from marsh, millstream, and river, until the orange light of midday brightens to gold, and at last the dying day passes away in one vast conflagration of purple and crimson and fiery red. So, too, it changes with the changing year. The golden summer deepens at length to the crimson and purple-brown of autumn and winter; the new year leaps into life in a sudden tide of green; then comes the triumph of spring, when cyclamen and hyacinth, harebell and convolvulus make the war-stained earth like the Garden of Paradise.

The Campagna again is not like the sea, which is dreadful because it remembers not: every bank and hillock has its remnant of tomb or villa or fortress, for this is a wilderness of ruin, a region of shallows which an ebbing tide of human greatness has left strewn with myth and legend; and here under haunted mound or riven tower sleep great cities which have sunk into the underworld, older capitals of Latium, cities which once were rich as Carthage, glorious as Athens, ancient as Tyre. Countless ages have passed since nature swept again over their ruins in a scarlet flame of poppies or a blue tide of April flowers, but the same eternal stream of life in leaf and blossom is waiting for the day when Rome too must go down in the abyss of time; when the red valerian shall flame upon the altars, green tapestries of matted ivy shall hang from pillar to pillar; when the climbing rose shall perfume the churches with its scented showers and the shrines shall be heaped up with treasure of golden broom; when the fading saints and martyrs shall be veiled by bacchanalian vine-wreaths, and the only music shall be the rustling of the reeds and the sighing of the grasses, the only worshippers a heavenly host of flowers.

It is strange what a sense of power and freedom these mighty outlooks give, lifting the mind high above all the pettinesses of life, like a night spent under the stars. For the spirit of man like his body abhors restraint and confinement, will not be pent up in a narrow compass nor be content without a spacious horizon in which the eye may wander and fancy and memory may move. There is narrowness and madness in these shut-in views of park and mill-stream and wooded hillside, and a palace to be fit for thinkers or rulers of men should look down upon a distant country where one may drink deep draughts of space and freedom, upon a bay studded with islands, or at least upon some great river which, like the stream of Time, bears onwards its freight of lives and treasure, of human hopes and fears.

This, then, leads up to what I believe to be the great secret of success in garden-making, the profound platitude that we should abandon the struggle to make nature beautiful round the house and should rather move the house to where nature is beautiful. It is only part of the garden which lies within the boundary walls, and a great scheme planned for dull or commonplace surroundings is a faulty conception, as if one were to propose to build half a house or to paint half a picture. The garden must be considered not as a thing by itself, but as a gallery of foregrounds designed to set off the soft hues of the distance; it is nature which should call the tune, and the melody is to be found in the prospect of blue hill or shimmering lake, or mystery-haunted plain, in the aerial perspective of great trees beyond the boundary, in the green cliffs of leafy woodland which wall us in on either hand. It may be argued further that real beauty is neither in garden nor landscape, but in the relation of both to the individual, that what we are seeking is not only a scenic setting for pool and fountain and parterre, but a background for life. Natural loveliness at the doors will give a hundred times more enjoyment than loveliness a mile away, and as in the earlier days when every one's parlour was under the sky, when the heath and forest and moorland stretched up to the walls of the city and the towers of the castle, health will follow in its train. A garden in a verdurous landscape which strikes a note of beauty and freedom, of exuberant fertility, of happy adaptation to the service of man, will be a nobler gift to the future, more fitted to survive; we shall share in the overflowing happiness of others, and the halo of associations being so much a part of the self that the two can never be disentangled, those who are near to us will shine in our eyes with a reflected light.

There is also to be considered the influence of

scenery upon mood and character, an influence so potent that being shown the surroundings of an ancient mansion, one seems to understand at a glance the lives of those who lived under its roof. There are some outlooks that stir the blood like the sound of a trumpet, and others that lull the senses to dreamy and indolent repose. Hamerton's theory is that born in every man is the need of some particular type of landscape, which will throw back to him the light of his own soul in grand or gay or sweet or melancholy beauty; that the lover of liberty will find delight in the vast horizons of the ocean and the desert, while the lover of tranquillity will sigh for the happy valley of Rasselas or the island lawns of Avilion; that restless energy will prefer the brown and rugged grandeur of Salvator Rosa and indolence or weakness will find repose in the golden peacefulness of Claude. Undoubtedly there is a difference between individuals. To some minds the Campagna is a dismal solitude, a fever-haunted desert, a nurse of terrible thoughts; to others it is a miracle of changing beauty, having just that background of melancholy which makes happiness more profound. But such a doctrine seems to allow too much to individual choice, too little to heredity and early impressions. The Highlander is as firmly wedded to grey boulder, black tarn, and boding rain cloud as the Dutch *boer* to his trim canals and flat alluvial plain – 'who', writes Tacitus of the earlier Germany, 'would live in such a wild and rugged country, were it not his fatherland?' The man is moulded by the landscape more often than the landscape is chosen by the man. Indeed, some great poets seem to have become one with their surroundings, giving expression – one might almost say consciousness – to the scenery of a particular district, as an orator gives back in flood the half-formed thoughts and aspirations which rise to him in vapour. Thus Wordsworth reflects the soft vales and shadowy hills and tranquil planes of light of the English lakes, Perugino the serene sweep of the blue Umbrian uplands. If, then, the landscape has such power over us that it may influence our very thoughts and being, that greatness of soul of which Longinus speaks should be sought not only in the companionship of great men, great books, and great pictures, but in looking upon the face of Nature in her grander moods.

The sublime is within the reach of few, the beautiful of many, for in countries such as Italy and Britain the diversity of scenic loveliness and local climate, of soil, rainfall, and vegetation, is almost beyond belief. In the north of Scotland there are gardens full of plants which at London would perish from the winter cold. In one Pem-

Isola Madre,
Lake Maggiore

brokeshire valley the verbena is a tree of shade, while half a mile away there are shrivelled oaks in a waste of gorse and heather. At Brindisi, the traveller may shiver on the quay in a December wind, while summer is still reigning in the Consul's garden across the harbour mouth. On Lake Maggiore, he may pass at Isola Madre into the Tropics, and look upon strange flowers and shrubs which are hardly to be seen elsewhere in Europe. He may find dismal solitudes, such as that great moor of Rannoch which Hamerton describes, where hundreds of square miles are given over to a chaos-world of blackness and bogs and muddy, melancholy sedges, with one long sinuous lake, dreary as Acheron; and scenes of beauty beyond the power of pen to picture or pencil to portray. Equally amazing are the contrasts of soil, for as there are desolate and blighted valleys where nature seems to lie under a curse; where the tree-forms are gnarled and stunted and nothing flourishes but deadly and ill-omened herbs; where the bushy nightshade is black with its poisonous berries, and gorgeous foxgloves, rank masses of hemlock and nettles, foul henbane, black mullein, and stinking horehound run riot as in a witches' garden; so there are happier lands which have come under a double blessing; where the stream of life in plant and tree flows with an added strength,

like a brook from the mountain pastures; where
the oaks make a mightier bole and giant buttresses
uphold the beeches; where the mossy slopes are
starred with primroses in spring and in autumn
the bracken rises breast-high in a tumbled sea of
green and russet-brown and tawny gold. Even for
a world-worn man such surroundings will lighten
labour and sorrow, will add to the brightness of
the sunny hours, and for a child whose senses are
yet unblunted, his whole being alive to every impression of beauty, they will heap up a treasury of
golden recollections which the Gods cannot take
away.

But if we are to seek natural beauty and to follow the senators of the Empire and the cardinals of
the Renaissance to the unfurrowed hills, we must
not be afraid to build, if occasion demands, high
on the mountain side, nor like Lucullus and the
storks and cranes to change our habitation with
the seasons. How many a modern architect, if such
a site as that of Mondragone were proposed to
him, would scout the suggestion, pointing out
that the place would be bitterly cold in the winter,
that the cost and labour of carrying up to it lug-
gage, fuel, and household supplies would be
intolerable; and so the matter would end in a
degrading compromise, the client submitting,
though sadly, to the superior judgement of his

professional adviser, and the house being placed half-way up the slope, where the views are hardly worth having, while the inconvenience is almost as great. The Italians of the sixteenth century were wiser than that; they knew the same house could not be expected to serve for both seasons of the year; they built for the summer *villeggiatura* and were content to spend Christmas in the town. These great villas at Frascati, Tivoli, and Albano were never intended for winter residence. At the present day many men of very moderate means indulge themselves with a summer cottage, and this example is likely to be followed by their richer and less intelligent neighbours, who have more than one residence, but lack the foresight to map out their lives. A house or garden which is expected to look fairly well all the year round can never reach the ideal, and the advantage of knowing during what months it will be occupied and of planning for those months alone is too obvious to be worth discussing.

Next to the choice of site, I would put the maxim that we must subordinate the house to the landscape, not the landscape to the house,[11] making it vast and austere where the note is one of grandeur or ruggedness; sweet and low where nature is in a smiling mood; tall in a level plain; rich with coupled shafts and sculptured friezes and cool colonnades if it faces a quiet prospect; great and dignified in a country of mighty trees. As the house must be related either by harmony or by contrast to the surrounding scenery, so the garden should be in sympathy with them both, the lines being broad and simple against a restless background of rolling hills and dales or where nature has a touch of the sublime, richer, fuller, and brighter against a peaceful setting of distant wooded slopes or purple mountains. The climax, as in a picture, may be in the foreground or may be in the background; but cannot be in both.[12] To the house the garden will be as intimately related, for it should be convenient as if one were 'stepping from one room to another,' and will often carry forward the main divisions or repeat the minor architectural features of the façade; will lay at the feet of the house its brightest gift of flowers and consider in the planning of vista and parterre the outlook from the windows. But the first aim of the designer will always be to consult the genius of the place, to catch the music of the landscape, and concentrate it by fitting foregrounds and the concealment of defects, whether it be the blue distance seen between the links of a low chain of hills, the shadowy gulf of a deep river-valley, or the green velvet of a mulberry-wooded plain, a view as at Amalfi along the limestone headlands

'Avenue of a Hundred Fountains', Villa d'Este, Tivoli

of an enchanted coast, or as at Monreale over a vale where the lemon is ripening in softest green and palest gold. If it be true that the connection with humanity is the principal interest of every landscape [3] and will best find expression in the foreground, then these garden outlooks are the most beautiful pictures in the world.

Having chosen a site and determined the relation of house and garden to the landscape and to each other, we may now consider more closely the inward meaning of our task. The garden, in every language, speaks of seclusion. To flower and plant and tree it is a cloistered refuge from the battle of life, a paradise where free from the pinch of poverty and the malice of their enemies, they may turn their thoughts and their strength from war to beauty; and this perfect freedom of the garden finds a voice in the joyous murmur of the fountain, for water too is outside the struggle for existence, and goes on its way rejoicing from one ocean of darkness to another. So, to man, the garden should be something without and beyond nature; a page from an old romance, a scene in fairyland, a gateway through which imagination lifted above the sombre realities of life may pass into a world of dreams. One should be able to escape to it from labour or business, from office or Senate-house or study, as to a haven of rest and refreshment, where Time does not dole out his seconds to you like a miser telling his guineas, nor snatch again the golden moments you cannot hold: no sound of the outer world should break the enchantment; no turret-clock should toll the passing hour; nor, could one silence it, should there vibrate through the garden the menacing voice of the church bell, with its muttered curse on nature and on man, lest it beat down the petals of the pagan roses.

All this would be easy enough if we were living in the age of Virgil the Enchanter, or Merlin, or King Roger of Sicily, or Albertus Magnus, or Michael Scott; a few woven circles upon the sand, an earth-shaking spell from the book, and there would be our enchanted fastness, high-walled like the Garden Mirth in the old romance against pale Sorrow and wrinkled Care and envious Time and all the spectres of the night. But in this unimaginative age, when a necromancer who ventures even to tell a fortune may be committed as a rogue and vagabond, it is necessary to be more circumspect; we must endeavour to find some form of 'white' magic which does not come within the meaning of the Act. In a garden, as elsewhere, Art has the power by selection, accentuation, grouping, and the removal of defects or superfluities, to intensify and surpass the beauty of nature, thus reaching the ideal.[13] This power, being higher than natural law, is a kind of witchcraft; but it is not the kind of which I speak. Art has another function also; it is concerned not only with the scene but with the mind of the beholder, for more than half of what we see comes from the mind. Here then at last we have found the garden-magic of Italy, in the domain of Psychology – that occult science which deals in spells, exorcisms, and bewitchments, in familiar spirits, in malign and beneficent influences and formulas of alchemy; that dim untrodden under-world from which Shakespeare and Wagner drew their shadowy legions, which will yet inspire the great poets, artists, and musicians of the age to come. If we use the witchery that here lies ready to our hand, the garden, like the work of a great painter, may 'create a mood'; may throw over the soul the spell of a persisting present, unpursued by a ravenous past, the child's illusion of an harmonious universe, free from the discords of sorrow or unkindness, from the dominion of iron Necessity or of scornful Chance; where forethought may colour the future with rainbow images of spring and hope, and memory like a fountain pool that has cast off the dark days of winter can reflect nothing but flowers and sunshine and deep-blue sky. We shall hear an echo of felicities older than mankind in the birds' most ancient song, shall know the thrill of numbers and see in the tender, tranquil eyes of the flowers, their drooping heads or pouted lips, other beings like ourselves who may return the sympathy we feel.[14]

We shall share with all living things that sense of union with nature which is the very essence of pleasure – in the radiant happiness of the plants whose flowering is the expression of a desire to live, a sigh of well-being, a smile of thankfulness, a hymn of praise, whose blossom is as laughter and whose perfume is as song, and the sight of all these smiling faces will teach us that life is a splendid gift, not a vale of tears but a dell of roses. We shall learn the philosophy of the plants, which have ceased from their wanderings, which do not seek to shiver in the cold shadow of impending ill, to groan in anticipation under evils which are beyond remedy and evils which may never arise, to guard against the future by building up an organ of instability, an organ of suffering, but have made their peace with Destiny, resigning themselves in hope and trustfulness to their winter sleep. We shall learn the inmost secrets of the garden, the hidden relations, the waves of mysterious affinity that flow between these flowers that cannot thrive except in the company of their kind, the green thoughts of the trees whose leaves are trembling at the sough of the distant rain, spring's first 'faint beatings in the calyx of the rose'. So, as time goes on, the glamour of the garden shall deepen, till we know that it is a commonwealth and that we are citizens with the rest. The great trees cast their shade over the garden, which shields them from the woodman's axe; man gives in labour what he takes in beauty, and every bush and flower has its appointed task, for there are some that feed the minstrels or find their dole of honey for the marriage-making bees, that watch through the midnight hours or guard the thickets with thorns and prickly blades and snares of coiling cables; and some there are that worship the Sun God, following in silent adoration his progress through the sky, and some that breathe a perfumed prayer at morn or even, when he scatters from his chariot the soft roses of dawn, or returns like a conqueror to his flaming city in the west. Thus it seems that one interest binds the garden together, one desire runs through it, a common purpose animates the whole: to dream through the dreary winter, when the petals of the cloud roses are drifting down in sheets of chilly blossom, when the boughs of the leafless woodland are heavy with crystal fruit, then, when the dream is over, to wake again, to creep out from the darkness, to bask in the sunshine of another year.

But if we are to call up this new world of mists and shadows to replace the illusions of the old, it will be necessary to face the problems of psychology and in the first place to analyse the pleasure which the beauty of a garden gives. There is no truth but the whole truth concerning an object, both in its countless aspects and manifold relations, and what we call the garden is only a single, fugitive appearance, an infinitesimal part of the whole; not a reality, but a phantom which we mistake for a reality. It is not even a part of the truth, all we know with certainty of such existences in the outer world being that in every quality and feature they are utterly unlike our conception of them. A rose is neither red nor sweet though we may think it so. To the old man, time and space and colour are not the same as they are to the boy. For the tiny creatures that swarm in a dewdrop and may swim in thousands through the eye of a needle, the garden has no existence; it is beyond the grasp of their minds, beyond the ken of their senses, further off than the clustering suns of the Milky Way. For the blind man it is a dull place; not a sight, but a sequence of touches with feet and hands, a succession of perfumes, of lightly echoed sounds, of the perception of obstacles and open spaces; a place of soft turf, warm sunshine, and whispering breezes. The thing itself with him is the chain of touches, the other impressions are only signs of the thing: if you could show him the garden he would not recognise it. For the smaller winged inhabitants of the flower-land, which make ten or fifteen thousand wing strokes in a single second and are supposed to be conscious of every one, time moves by another measure, the day is a twelve-month long and gravity a restraint as light as it may be to the dwellers upon Mars. To their eyes, which reach beyond the violet rays, the world is full of colour which we may not see, to their ears of rhythms which we may not hear, calls and love-songs and shrill alarms and rustling music of unfolding leaves and pistol-shots of bursting bud or falling berry; and other senses they may have [4] which the heart cannot even conceive, differing from ours as light from heat or sound from motion. They indeed must find it such a wonderland as we have dreamed, an en-chanted forest of fearful delights, where trees a thousand feet high are laden with flowers of in-credible magnificence, roses great as arbours, snowy cupolas and purple obelisks, spires of red-crocketed blossom, peals of azure bells; with cup-like flowers that offer fairy foods – ambrosia, and draughts of nectar and chalices of poison; where skiffs with painted sails come floating down the breeze, and nets of corded silk are gemmed with globes of rainbow crystal, and in the green light of the thickets lurk forms of unearthly beauty or of uttermost horror – dragons in jewelled mail or burnished armour, horned dinosaurs, and filthy creeping monsters; where the flying moments flow with a soft gliding, like weary watches of the night, and giant magicians pass onward with imperceptible motion, slow as the snowy clouds that steal through the summer sky.[15]

To human beings, from whom all these marvels are hid, the beauty of a garden is less enthralling, the pleasure less acute. It is what is termed a massive and soothing pleasure, built up of many strands of feeling. There is the pride of the eye in colour and curving lines and dappled light and shade; the suggestion of pleasing rest and coolness; the intellectual pleasure of the processes of comparison and deduction: the train of association which calls up memories of other gardens, of other trees and flowers; the appeal to the sympathetic sentiments of power and happiness,[16] whereby we rejoice in another's good fortune, finding delight in the vigour and well-being of plant and herb and tree. Further, there is the gratification of the instinctive sympathy of reason, where the scene has the qualities of appropriateness, diversity in unity, proportion, symmetry or balance, orderly progression, all of which come under the head of design, or at least of order and fitness. In every well-planned garden, as indeed in every work of art, there are many harmonies of appropriateness – in relation, convenience, proportion or scale, form, colour, historic style – so subtle as to escape individual notice;[17] but these come within the halo of obscurely felt relations, and being fused together rise above the threshold of consciousness in a vague and general sense of ordered beauty. Art's highest appeal to emotion is in the region of subconsciousness.

Up to this point we have dealt only with the impressions which reach us through the avenue of sight, but the influence of the other senses in a garden is not so trifling as might at first appear. It has often been observed how the impressiveness of natural scenery is heightened by some sound in harmony with the landscape, by the scream of the eagle in the mountains, the howling of wolves in the forest, by the goatherd's piping, the carols of harvest home, the song of the nightingale, the trembling music of the vesper bell. Alison considers such sounds to be sublime[18] or beautiful only from association, the mind connecting them with certain qualities and certain scenes: but the power they have over us would rather seem to be due to the suggestion of life and force and movement, to the tightened grip of reality, the shock of surprise, to something which nature here uses with a success beyond the reach of orator or rhetorician – the device of impersonification. The landscape, as you gaze upon it, has found a sudden voice. It is speaking – telling you the wild delight of savage freedom, the fervour of the chase, the careless Eden of the upland pastures, the thankfulness of harvest, the rapture of requited love, the tranquil sadness of the dying day. So lofty a string of emotion may not be stirred in a garden, where sublimity, if it be reached at all, can only be the sublime of nature beyond the boundaries; but the peaceful murmur of a fountain placed at the climax of the scene may heighten its prevailing note, the rush of water will give life, and statue or fountain masks may add the crowning interest of personality. Other sounds and the stirrings of other senses – the warbling of birds, the sighing of the wind in the tree-tops, the myriad-tongued murmur of the lime-blossoms, the perfumes of free-scented flowers, the soft and springy turf, warm sun, and breaths of vagrant air – each of these has its share in building up the impression we receive.[19]

The eyes, owing to the variety of their functions and the power of dealing with many objects at once, must always be the dominant sense, but being on duty for fully sixteen hours out of the twenty-four, they are apt to fall into a kind of

waking slumber. The ear, on the other hand, has
so much leisure that it is alive to every sound, and
having originally been employed to give warning
of danger, as is shown by the infant's fear of noise,
it instantly awakes the mind. Thus aroused, the
brain uses the eyes to greater advantage, selecting
among a countless multitude of new impressions
those which bear upon the subject of thought.
The sense of smell has also its peculiar province,
a strange power of conjuring up the past,[20] being
bound up with memory because at some early
stage of racial development it has been, like the
sense of taste, necessary for the protection of life:
and we shall therefore carry away a lasting recollection of the garden, if round the fountain of
which we have spoken the air is heavy with the
scent of some particular flower, or succession of
flowers, if 'the woodbine spices are wafted abroad
and the musk of the rose is blown'. But the chief
work of the other senses in a garden is to heighten
the feeling of reality, without which we cannot
really understand nor know nor enter into possession, for as in reading and even in thinking we
are assisted to grasp the meaning of the symbols
by mental images of the feeling of articulation
and of the sound of the words, so these sensory
impressions of sound, scent, and touch tighten
our grasp of the object and, adding the criterion

Fountain,
Villa Lante,
Bagnaia

of reality, the power to inflict pleasure or pain, make it part of the one ultimate fact, the consciousness of our own existence. With the eyes a double impression at slightly varying angles gives a striking perception of solid effect, and how much stronger is the conviction of truth when we have approached the scene from so many, from such widely different sides; when the senses in conjunction, like a party of experts in a laboratory, have tested it for light, colour, form, motion, space-distribution, distance, and magnitude; for the freshness of the air, the chemical constituents of flower and grass and tree; for the signs of sunshine, wind, and turf; for the intensity, the volume, continuance, tone, clearness, harmony, rhythm, character of the sounds, and the evidence they give of distance, direction, and movement.

Thus the other organs of sense combine to strengthen belief and possession, to heighten the enjoyment of the eyes; pleasure gives an added force to energy and vitality, and the whole man is more alive; beauty rouses emotion, emotion unlocks the door to imagination, which is set free to wander in a world of dreams. Thus in the flowing tide of happiness, which has as much power to intensify reality and impressionability as melancholy has to diminish them [5] the constraints of trouble or preoccupation or self-consciousness are swept away, and following the general law that one great pleasure fires all the pleasurable sensibilities, the delights of the intellect, of society, music, poetry, even of food, exercise, and rest, are nowhere so vivid as in a garden. The golden lesson of Psychology is among the many selves to choose the best, and in such surroundings a new character is put upon the individual, sympathy is exalted, all the powers of the mind are at their brightest, and the acuteness of feeling is in itself a joy. Ruskin [6] and Alison make too much of raising a train of imaginative thought, which may heighten but cannot cause the enjoyment of beauty that we feel at the first glance; and indeed the delight which landscape gives is due chiefly to the elevation of mood, lifting the mind out of those gloomy realms where sorrow and suffering or disappointment or anxious foreboding have gathered round them the spectres of past unhappiness, above this object universe of double-faced pleasure and pain, to a world of sunshine where Beauty reigns over the shadows of the happy hours, and every shadow is a friend.

I
t will be asked perhaps what scientific basis
there is for all these pretty theories, and in
order to prove that the danger is not that one
should be too imaginative but that one should not
be imaginative enough, I must turn for a moment
to the physical process of which consciousness is
the other side. The higher centres of sensation in
the cerebral hemispheres are storehouses of old
impressions [7] and those which have often been
in action together become connected [8]: we have
therefore, answering to each cluster of qualities
and relations frequently met with in the outer
world, an organised group or *plexus* of cells and
fibres in the brain, of which if any part is stirred
the wave of nervous excitement will tend to spread
to the rest. Let a fresh cluster of a kind already
known unexpectedly, offer itself – say the view of
a garden – and the recognition of it as belonging
to a particular class will involve the faint revival
in memory or idea of (i) the aggregate of past impressions, and (ii) the knowledge grouped about
them; in this case all that gardens have meant to
countless generations of human beings, the flower
language of love, flowers as the universal symbol
of beauty and motive of ornament, the pathos of
the faded rose, the Idyll of Ausonius and Ben Jon-

son's rendering of it, the garden lore of Herrick, Vaughan, and Herbert, the flower imagery of Milton and Shakespeare, of Keats and Shelley. These ideas, or others like them, will be in the background of consciousness [9] not in the focus of intellectual sight but in the 'fringe' or 'halo' of obscurely felt relations; belonging rather to feeling than to knowledge [10]; below the horizon themselves, but rolling up above it a mist of sentiment out of which at any moment trains of conscious thought may spring.

This is not all. The centres which deal with sensation and emotion being the same, a faint stirring of past experiences involves also a more vivid renewal of (iii) the emotion common to such past experiences and (iv) of other feelings of pleasure which have been accidentally associated with them.[21] In our garden melody of delight we have thus in addition to the gratification which is found in the exercise of eye and ear and brain, in the prospect of investigation and comparison, in the calling up past impressions crowned with a garland of sentiment and knowledge, and the troupe of pleasurable emotions which dance attendance upon them, – the echo of a counterpart; a re-representation of the fresh gladness of spring, the joy and wonder of a child's heart, the ease and freedom of other hours spent in the garden, the happiness experienced in the companionship of parents, playmates, and friends, sympathy felt in the pleasure of others; and beyond these chords, mysterious overtones, fainter echoes from the immeasurable past, dim ancestral reminiscences of emotions stirred by the freer life of mountain and river, of the forest and of the chase [11]. Even this is not all, though already the process goes beyond comprehension and almost beyond belief. The reproduction in idea of past feelings tends to revive, not only others accidentally connected with them, but (v) all others of the same class [12]. So, the masses of plexuses in the brain which deal with impressions intermixed with pleasurable emotion being intimately connected and the nervous discharge following the lines of least resistance, other feelings of beauty and happiness are partially aroused, there is a dim representation, vague, massive, multitudinous, of all kinds of pleasure, and an indefinable sense of well-being [13].

To these delights of a garden age may add a further interest which can hardly be distinguished from beauty, for the mind, at least with those who have the historic instinct, is always longing to be connected with the past, and dreading for itself confinement upon the plane of time, delights in evidences of the long continuance of nations, families, and institutions, in hale and vigorous old age, in long-settled peace beyond the turn of Fortune's wheel, the 'scornful dominion of Accident'. Restfulness is the prevailing note of an old garden; in this fairy world of echo and suggestion where the Present never comes but to commune with the Past, we feel the glamour of a Golden Age, of a state of society just and secure which has grown and blossomed as the rose. How few there are who are incapable of feeling the mysterious appeal of such a place – of the scenes which reflect upon the passion and the happiness of bygone generations, the statues which gleam out under the deepening spell of the twilight like phantoms of old-world greatness, the still pools that slumber in the sunshine and call our spirits to their dreamland of abiding peace, the rippling music of the fountain, like trills of elfin laughter, and the hoarse watervoices that are hasting with passionate earnestness to the everlasting sea. But beyond all this there is a deeper mystery. In such scenes there is the same elusive suggestiveness that is found in the perfume of the flowers. That which is interesting is real [14], and the old garden is very real. It has the power of fixing attention, it grips you by the sleeve, it is instinct with a silent eloquence; you feel in the Spiritualist phrase that it is 'seeking to communicate', to open vistas into the past, that it has a secret to unfold, a message to deliver. What

Palazzo Borromeo,
Isola Bella,
Lake Maggiore

then is this secret of the old-world garden? This —
that it knows us well. We have come back to an
earlier home, to scenes which are strangely familiar to us, to the life of former generations whose
being was one with ours. Every living creature is
adapted to its environment by changes in brain
structure produced either by the natural selection
of accidental variations or by multitudinous repetition of the same impressions and the same
actions. It is this harmony with the surroundings
which we feel upon entering an old house or garden; vague ancestral memories are faintly stirred[22]
and the sentiment which may attach to objects that
have been habitual sources of enjoyment to generation after generation [15]. If by long hereditary
connection pleasure has thus become associated
with a child's doll [16], it may be with a flower
or even with a garden; and more particularly with
a garden that represents the ideal world of our
forefathers, reflecting the care and forethought,
the high unselfish endeavour, the ordered symmetry, the simple quaint formality of their lives.
Architecture, far more than poetry or any of the
sister arts, is a 'strong conqueror of the forgetfulness of men'. History and romance may leave us
cold and unconvinced – the past of which we read
or hear is far away; but let the primordial sense of
touch extended by sight be brought into action,

with its stronger grip of reality,[23] its greater precision, its fuller information – let our hands handle and our eyes behold the homes of our ancestors, and instantly we are back in the life of earlier days. We are dealing no longer with mental images – homeless wanderers in the world of space disowned and rejected by all around – but with the thing itself; thoughts which are almost memories flash upon the mind, a host of associated facts take their places in the scene, and before us there rises the majestic pageant of the past.

It has been observed of the sham rivers introduced into English parks by Capability Brown, that when once the two ends have been discovered, they have lost for ever their beauty and their power to please. As continuance is part of the idea of a river, so it is of a garden, and no new pleasure-ground will satisfy the mind unless we may see it both as it is and as it is to be, when the hedges have shot up into fortress walls of green, and flowering weeds have rooted themselves in the crannies, and the lichen is creeping over the balustrades in a slow tide of curdled foam; when the robes of Nymph and Naiad are damasked with gold and silver blooms, and old associations are gathering in the garden, thickly as autumn leaves. A garden, like a building, must be stable in appearance as well as in reality, must have the restfulness of assured position; the glory of youth is in its promise as of age in its memories. If the scheme has no air of permanence, no wall of defence against the gipsy horde of briars and brambles which is waiting to break into the forbidden land, to pitch its tents on the paths, and riot over the lawns, and pluck down the flower-vases; if it mourns an unsettled or a gluttonous age, which takes no heed of the morrow; if it despairs of the future, preaching the uncertainty of life and the uselessness of effort – the cup of beauty it offers will be tainted with sadness. In our flower-fastness there must be solid evidence of lime and stone that the labour of the builder has been for others; for after-generations who shall mix its music with their joys and sorrows, with their hopes of the future and their memories of the past.

Whenever we look at a picture, we are entering a new world of imagination, leaving the real and turning to the ideal. So it should be with a garden, and to proclaim it boldly as a kingdom of romance we may people it with figures of Olympian deities, with virtues and graces, wood-nymphs and dell-nymphs, dryads and satyrs. Even the topiary works of the Renaissance, the green ships and helmets, giants, dragons and centaurs, had something of reason to recommend them, for by their very strangeness they would be likely to compel attention, to stir imagination, to strengthen memory, to banish the consciousness of self and all trivial or obsessing thoughts. The frontiers of this fairy kingdom must be clearly marked by ramparts strong enough to prevent intrusion, but not in such a way as to shut out the distant landscape. One of the great lessons of psychology is the importance of trifles, and when all our labour is done we may find the eye returning again and again, not to fountain or lawn or parterre, but to some object so trivial that it can be hidden by a single finger of the outstretched hand; some tiny cloud of blue which tells of a far-off mountain, some gleam of distant water half seen between the trees, or green depth of a forest glade. The fascination of such sights, whether due to the excitement of wonder, the ancestral call of wild nature [17], or the charm of mystery in a landscape where something should always be left to fancy and to desire [18], is too strong to be resisted; the whole lay-out should be subordinated to them, and on no account should they be cut off by a rigid boundary, the 'good high wall for choice' of the English architects.

The garden, like every other work of art, should have a climax, which may be emphasised by moving water or by reflection, by higher light and deeper shadow, by colour, elaboration in design, or by sculpture which adds the charm of personality;

and whatever this focus of interest may be, whether
it stirs the emotion of sublimity by the prospect of
mountain amphitheatre or plunging cataract or
measureless infinity of plain, the emotion of beauty
by immemorial cypresses, by lake or river valley,
blue pool or fountain basin, it must be presented
with what is known as 'economy of the recipient's
attention' [19]; that is to say, without the addition
of features which disturb or detract. If a picture be
complete, everything that is added is something
taken away. The Law of Novelty will teach us not
to fritter away the effect in half glimpses, but to
deliver it with unsullied freshness, like a knock-
down blow straight between the eyes; for it is a
fundamental principle that no second occurrence
of any great stimulus can ever be fully equal to the
first. The power of novelty to 'quicken observation,
sharpen sensation and exalt sentiment' [20] is as
marked as that of familiarity to throw a veil over
ugliness [21]. Surprise may add to novelty the shock
of contradiction, and if care has been taken to make
the expectation less than the reality, we shall have
the added thrill of wonder. Indeed, in every great
garden there should be some element of wonder
or surprise, if only to make recollection more vivid
[22]. We shall learn, again, from the Law of Relativ-
ity that as the emotions of beauty, sublimity, novelty, and freedom represent in each case a change

in consciousness from the less to the more pleasing, so either of them may be heightened by contrast, that is to say, according to circumstances, by an ugly, commonplace, monotonous, or confined approach. In the opposition of sunshine to the coolness of shade and water, another principle is involved, for the actual bodily discomfort heightens reality, and the mind attaching little value to that which has cost it nothing, we shall do well, though Bacon is against us, to buy our shade by passing through a few yards of sun. Contrast again may take another form which brings it under the head of harmony; that is to say, the opposition to each other of pleasing qualities which it thereby makes more distinct and noticeable, as of lofty terrace to low parterre, of studied order to wayward negligence, of massive strength to tender grace.

Such a harmony of contrast is especially valuable at the garden boundary. For this reason the mossy pillars of the woodland, where it beats against the garden, are to be wreathed with a wild tangle of ivy and vine, of hop or honeysuckle or convolvulus, and the trees themselves to be such as affect a rough and rugged form, gnarled oaks with a hydrabrood of writhing arms or rugged elms or knotty chestnuts; for this reason we are to avoid a multiplication of enclosures, which destroys the background of the picture, throwing back too far from the house the contrast between the wild riot of rebellious nature and the Roman peace of art. Bacon's gardens of the months may be suited to the promenades of a city park, but are not to a private nor even to a royal garden. If spaciousness is desired, it will best be obtained by carrying forward the axial line, or main alley, along a canal or cascade or *tapis vert* of green turf, a plan equally appropriate for the manor-house and for the palace.

Straight lines, according to Ruskin, are valuable because they suggest restraint and set off by their monotony the freedom and variety of natural curves: it follows that flowers will be fairer in formal beds, wild foliage when opposed to massive masonry. Indeed, irregularity and diversity naturally confuse and bewilder us, having no beauty of their own, but only by contrast with a background of order and unity. Symmetry, which gives a sense of rest, will be the law of the garden, the human mind being prejudiced in favour of simplicity and rhythmic recurrence [23], but symmetry too exact is a characteristic of dead rather than of living things, as in the latter it is never quite perfect and is disguised by movement. With gardens, as with buildings, life and freedom are given to the plan by slight aberrations from the square which can hardly be perceived unless they are sought for

[24]. It is surprising how much real freedom is wrapped up in the old formality. The circular endings of the terraces at Hampton Court and Helmsley conceal the awkward return of the paths which run into them. The star-shaped parterre in the Colonna garden at Rome covers a corner entrance. The plans of Caserta, Palazzo Borghese, Isola Bella, the Vatican, and Boboli gardens, Levens and Melbourne in England, show how easy it is to disguise a change of direction. At Villa d'Este the designer has twisted the great descent of his central alley some yards to the left, caring little that the squalid houses of the town should encroach upon the corner of his garden and even cross its middle line. At Fenarola, a late eighteenth-century garden near Brescia, a bolder divergence from rectitude is concealed by what one can only describe as a heartless fraud. Behind the house is a formal ascent on the hillside, interrupted in the centre by an octagon, the lower flights of steps being steeper than those above, so that it is impossible to see both series at once. Within this octagon, masked by the sweep of a double stairway, the axial line changes very considerably, to suit the plane of the higher hillside; but the visitor only discovers the trick on the high road, half a mile from the house, and drives away with an uncomfortable feeling that the architect has been laughing at him.

Of statues in the garden, Bacon has written that they are for state and magnificence, but nothing to the true pleasure of it; and Temple could see little in them, or rather in the stone of which they are made, beyond a suggestion of coolness in the summer heat; yet from this faint and damning praise we may appeal to Wagner's great rule that as far as possible all the arts should be used in conjunction, and to Spencer's judgment that the highest æsthetic feeling is roused by the exercise of many powers [25]. Let sculpture add yet another appeal to emotion, and the pleasure stirred by beauty in a garden may rise from massive to acute. It is not only that the statues will set off the garden; we have to consider also that the garden will set off the statues, crowning them with a garland of beauty they could not have elsewhere. Further, there is the opinion already so much insisted upon, that the designer should aim at the ideal, not merely at that low form of ideality which goes beyond nature in the perfection of shape and colour and arrangement, of leaf and blossom, turf and tree, but at the nobler kind that mixes imagination with beauty, taking us into a new world of romance out of all relation to experience and knowledge. In a modem picture-gallery, nothing is so refreshing as to turn from the dreary realism of modern landscapes to scenes whose character is boldly asserted by imaginary figures of satyrs or water-nymphs or centaurs. The original function of imagination seems to have been to prepare us in childish play for the battle of life and in manhood to enable us to foresee and guard against future dangers, and like other useful faculties this requires exercise and pays for it in pleasure. There is thus a natural emotion or passion of ideality, which craves to be satisfied, and every man in his own way must seek the ideal, whether he find it in church or library, in art or music or literature, in the cell of the monastery or the cave of the recluse, or in that flowery land where beauty has forgathered from the very ends of the earth.

This grown-up playfulness of the imagination finds encouragement in the fact that mankind, who spend a third of their lives in dreamland, give also much of their waking hours to imaginary worlds – to the world of appearances, the world of wrong ideas and popular errors and superstitions in which they cannot fail to believe, the various worlds of religion, more real in sickness than in health, the worlds of romance, which they only pretend to believe in. Imagination loves to be employed, and is so absorbed in the interest of ideal relations that it will shut its eyes to minor discrepancies, if only we can avoid the affront of an unnecessary contradiction; pleasure again helps to occupy the mind with the object, excluding all hostile influences. We do not see the unnatural lighting in the picture, the supporting blocks in the sculpture, the audience that sits about us: we are not even surprised when great Cæsar on the stage declaims in modern English. These enchanted scenes of theatre, opera, and academy do not actually command belief, but are real to us while we look upon them with the reality of similitude which has not reached its highest point; exact equality; for reality is only an assertion by the senses and the perception that the object belongs to the outer world of existence and is what it appears to be, while belief is a settled judgement that such an assertion is true. Consciousness of the outer world is a very complex thing, depending upon the excitation, not of a single centre, but of a great group or plexus of nerve cells and fibres which varies with every object, and some of these centres may be actually deluded, while in others the sensibility is only partial or latent. The mind cannot deal with more than one idea at a time, though three or four others may lurk in the background of consciousness. Somewhere in the very plexus occupied in putting before us an impression of the scene, is a brain tract which, if fully irradiated, will present us with the profound reflection that all these things are only painted shows; but its protests have been scouted, its warnings have been disregarded, it has been lulled to sleep.

But to return to the question of sculpture. Statuary proclaiming the imaginative ideal may strike in the garden a keynote of wonder and romance. The only rules it is necessary to observe are that there should be a background of mystery and obscurity, such as a forest or a great plain or a chain of distant mountains may give; a well-defined boundary; a shock of delight or surprise to lift us over the threshold of fact; an air of grandeur or distinction in the garden itself and in all its parts [26]; that we should not mix the worlds of romance, but should admit only one supernatural, other circumstances being congruous with it and with each other; that we should leave as much as possible to the mind, because imagination flies from a finished picture and loves to accept a bare suggestion [27], filling in the details for itself. But even where conditions do not favour the ideal, a pleasure-ground, however small, should have its presiding genius, its Nymph of flower-garden or grove or woodland, or Naiad of the Well, appealing to that other emotion of personality [28] which induces the mind to be ever looking for some being like itself, some face among the rocks or figure in the branching wood, to give a personal interpretation to the forces of nature and to feel in lake or mountain or forest the thrill of a living presence. This emotion, springing perhaps from the primal dread of solitude, forms a fresh bond between man and nature, enlarging the human interest and adding to the appreciation of natural beauty; and for this reason sculpture in a garden is to be regarded not as an ornament but almost as a necessity, as like that last touch of colour in a picture which sets the whole canvas in a flame [29].

Statues of marble seldom look well in Italy, never in England, and of all discords none can be so jarring as to place among the flowers dreadful forms of disease and suffering, cripples, or beggars, or the monstrous dwarfs that look down from the Valmarana garden[24] as if to symbolise the starved and stunted life of the wall-coping. Art, like laughter, should be the language of happiness, and those who suffer should be silent. Time and Care may wait without the gateway, but Time the ungracious guest, who is always late for the wedding feast and early for the funeral – envious Time, the spoiler of the roses, who lays his hateful scythe to the root of the fairest flowers, should have no image, no altar, in the garden, for it is by events and not by the measure of them that we grow old, and hours spent in a garden are stolen from Death and from Time. Only health and strength and beauty are at home among the flowers, shepherds and shepherdesses, youths and maidens in the garb of long ago, portly noblemen in periwigs and armour, warriors and Amazons, nymphs and satyrs, virtues and graces. We may personify the particular place in a figure or bust, taught by the gate at Capua and the pulpit at Ravello,[25] or commemorate an historic event by reference as in the cavalier's garden at Norton Conyers where a leaden warrior speaks discreetly of the Edgehill fight. We may represent the great elemental forces of nature, the higher motives which sway the human drama, the hoped-for triumph of Love over Death. We may build in some secluded nook a Cupid's altar, where many generations of lovers shall carve their names and make their offerings of flowers, or may set in the four quarters of the garden our pageant of the Seasons: Spring, as a winged youth, primrose-crowned, with flute and flower-embroidered robe; proud Summer as a weary king; spendthrift Autumn with open purse and lifted cup and gathered fruit; hoary Winter having a sealed casket under his foot, his beard hung with icicles and his mantle broidered with double-faced jests. No statue, however bad, should be condemned to a desolate old age. In a decorative landscape the figures are never happy unless they are enjoying themselves, and in a portrait

89

even ugliness is rendered charming by the presence of a child, a dog or bird. Diana in a garden should not be without her hound, nor Neptune without his sea-monster; Mars may be mated with Venus, Flora with Vertumnus, Cupid with Psyche; every Amazon should have her warrior and every nymph her satyr.

I have left almost to the last the magic of water, an element which owing to its changefulness of form and mood and colour and to the vast range of its effects is ever the principal source of landscape beauty, and has like music a mysterious influence over the mind. It was, perhaps, of this that Wagner was thinking when he wrote that music is like a power of nature which men perceive but do not understand. In the sound of rushing or of falling water there is beauty of reflection, for it repeats and by repeating deepens the joy or sorrow of the listener's mood; but to those who hearken more intently water will speak with a voice of its own, a message of peace or strength or freedom, in the careless timeless ease of its flowing, the lulling monotony of rhythmic sound, the exhilaration of power. But its chief appeal is through the avenue of sight. Movement representing to the eye the essential character of living things,[26] the quality by which they reveal themselves, just as inanimate objects are recognised by form, a foun-

Principal Fountain, Villa Lante, Bagnaia

tain or rivulet will be to the garden a well of living water. On the other hand, the reflections in
still basins have a strangely restful effect. They are
associated, as Ruskin points out [30], with the
idea of quiet succession and continuance; that
one day should be like another, one life the echo
of another life, being a result of quietude, part of
that great rhythm of harmonious change through
birth and death to birth again which is the heart-
beat of the universe. In lake or pool or river, water
emphasises the prevailing note of the landscape,
harmonises the picture by distributing or echoing
colours and forms, by 'reviving' the tints of sky,
foliage, and flowers, and whether in movement
or repose it fascinates the eye which returns to it
again and again; it should therefore, both in park
and garden, be found at the focus of beauty and
interest. These water reflections are actually more
delightful than the views they repeat [31], in the
softness of the lights, the depth, transparency and
intricacy of the shadows, the freshness and tender-
ness of the colouring; for the gloss of the water-
film is like the coat of old varnish which mellows
a picture; like the twilight it gives breadth, connection and unity; and the reversal of the image [32]
by baffling perception makes the colours richer
and the contrasts of light and shade more conspic-
uous. The effect goes even further than this. We

have not merely an improved presentment but an altered composition. The landscape is repeated from a fresh point of view, that is to say from one as much below the surface of the water as the spectator is above it, and all the objects which make it up are seen under different lights and in different relative positions. It may thus happen that the foreground, instead of being merged in soft meadow or shadowy foliage, is silhouetted upon the sky; is relieved, as in Turner's drawing of Nottingham [33], not against the dark base of a hill but against its sunlit summit. The middle distance is cut out of the picture, there is a sharper gradation of values from the nearer to the more distant reflections, and the shadows are not merely a lower tone but spaces of an entirely different hue, to which the heightened power of reflection gives depth and variety. The blue of the sky is darkened and other colours are altered or omitted. If there is the least movement of the surface, vertical lines will be lengthened and rendered more emphatic, while horizontal lines will tend to disappear.

But the distant view in a water landscape can never be so beautiful as a simple rendering of reeds and foliage. The grandest effect of all is produced by formal canals, not too large, which reflect the pavilion at the further end and the lime avenues which hedge them in. For smaller pools, the first object must be to give the water-artist something to play with – richly carved balustrades as at Frascati with fountain masks of bearded river-gods that drop tiny runlets of crystal into the basin, or mossy crevices, or the golden bloom of lichened stone, or plants, if any such exist, whose leaves are dark above and light below. Baby faces may lean to meet the reflections or, as in D'Annun-zio's novel, Love and Death may kiss each other. The larger or more vertical the angle at which one looks down, the greater is the difference between the scene and its echo [34]: we may thus, by slightly sinking the pool, reflect beauties of carv-ing and surface invisible from above; phantom forms may reveal themselves, or sculptured figures in the water may be springing up to grasp the shadows. The effect may be complicated by strange effects of light admitted through a crevice between bank and balustrade.

In water the two pictures always contend, re-flection and transparency being in inverse ratio to each other, and in some positions it may be better to abandon the surface and cultivate the beauties of the underworld. With a fountain basin, sculp-ture must necessarily be above the water, but in dealing with a still reservoir no such law is im-posed upon us. We may have a merman's pool, fringed with floating lilies, where below the water-film are sea-maidens and gold-red fish and under-water palaces, and that strange power the eye has of clearing away reflections by the change to a longer focus will enhance the effect by a sudden thrill of surprise. Columns and opposing mirrors may give endless vistas of pillared halls, and if the pool is near the upper edge of a cliff a strange light may be thrown into it through an opening protected by glass. We may build up a dark screen of masonry behind it and illuminate it through a water passage from a pool beyond, or make the still more interesting experiment of 'total internal reflection' [35], admitting the sun's rays in the late afternoon between the stems of a great hedge of beech or ilex at such an angle that the return-ing rays will lie along or actually under the sur-face of the water. Some of these will appear to be bizarre suggestions, and indeed it is likely enough that, except in great conservatories or winter gar-dens, under-water mirrors may produce an un-quiet effect. But until such experiments have been tried, an opinion is of little value. There are no rules in art which some great artist has not shown us how to break with advantage, and every new adventure is a voyage of discovery, the outcome of which no man may foresee. Nature has 'thou-sands of exquisite effects of light which are absolutely inexplicable', which can be believed only while they are seen, and by good fortune we may reap a larger harvest than we have sown.

Elsewhere the designer may prefer to play with the colour of water, seeking to reproduce those lovely hues of blue and green which the Italians of an earlier age caught and fixed in garden reservoirs, and even in small fountain basins. Water absorbs the red rays of the spectrum and is therefore a blue transparent medium, its colour when distilled being a tint of Prussian blue, as may be seen in the pure ice of the glacier crevasses. All that is necessary to bring out the natural beauty of the element by transmitted light is, firstly, a flood of strong sunshine; secondly, to look down from above as nearly vertically as possible; thirdly, to cut off reflections of the sky by trees or hedges or other dark objects. Suspended particles of glacier dust or chalk or lime add much to the brilliance of the effect, and in a country where the stone is red or yellow should give a tint of green or purple or violet. In England one may sometimes see blue or green pools at the bottom of a deserted stone-quarry: if experiment should show that good colour is unattainable at a higher level under these grey skies, we shall be justified in helping it out by the use of coloured tiles.

On the actual technics of garden-making volumes have been written, and I have no wish to add to the number. But there are still a few points which seem to have escaped attention. It should not be forgotten that there will always be one favourite or 'set' view of house and garden. This may be worked up to, as an artist composes a picture, with water reflections and re-entering curves, studied masses of light and shade, the repetition of harmonious lines and forms, and especially with such a handling of scale, perspective, values, and gradations of tone, as will enlarge rather than diminish the appearance of space and distance. With a new-built house, symbolic sculpture in the foreground may add the dignity of a larger meaning, and to an old hall that is yet unspoilt, broken fountain and weed-grown pavement may give the Pathos of Time. In addition to the 'set' view, the route to be followed by visitors who are shown over the place should be considered as carefully as by Louis XIV at Versailles, a great part of the enjoyment of a garden lying in the power to give pleasure to others and to share the pleasure of one's friends.

One of d'Argenville's four maxims was always to make the ground look larger than it really is. This principle must not be carried too far. We should aim, as he tells us in another place, at that which is great and noble and studiously avoid the

manner that is mean and pitiful, 'not making little Cabinets and Mazes, Basins like Bowl-dishes
and Alleys so narrow that two Persons can scarce
go abreast in them; choosing rather to have but
two or three things somewhat large, than a dozen
small ones which are no more than very trifles'.
Yet undoubtedly a slight increase in the apparent
size of the garden and, what is at least equally important, of the house, will add to the effect, and
in any case we must be careful not to fall into the
common fault of making them look smaller than
they are. There are many little tricks of technique
by which scale may be given. Every architect
knows how converging lines, lowered steps and
balustrades, slight successive reductions in the
size and distance apart of statues, obelisks, vases,
or other objects which repeat themselves, will
lengthen the perspective. A curious illusion of
spaciousness is produced in some of Knyff's en-
gravings of old English gardens by a number of
yew obelisks placed at equal intervals from each
other. With a small and simple house and garden
in a town, quite a good effect may be produced
by a false scale, if the owner accepts it as a convention and is determined to be amused by the
contradiction when giant figures come upon the
scene. D'Argenville's maxim should be reversed
when dealing with the approach to any building

of importance, and the architect should follow the precedents of Hardwick, Caserta, and of that villa at Pratolino which was described as being 'contemptible when seen from afar, but very fine when you come near it'; for as in the garden appearance should be greater than reality, so at the first view of the house expectation should be less than reality.

A principle which cannot be carried too far is Le Nôtre's law of contrast. It is not enough to consider this in the first rough scheme of the garden, in the general opposition of terraces to a great plain or of a broad flowery level to a landscape of rolling hills; we must apply it also at the boundary, where art and nature meet, and in every corner of the grounds, grouping together sunshine and shadow, grove and bowling-green, high and low, rich and simple, line and curve. In order to heighten the values of surfaces by contrast, every country house should have its paved court, its parterres of turf and gravel. The delicious softness of grass gives at the first footstep a release from care, which should be proffered close to the house, and if possible at a centre of beauty. Parterres of box and gravel have, independent of contrast, a peculiar dignity and beauty; it is not true, though often stated by English designers, that the Italians of the Renaissance would have preferred to use grass had the climate allowed. The colour and smooth surface of lemon-pots make a pleasant harmony with a box parterre, as stone vases and paving with a carpet of turf; indeed, in a green garden the walks should always be paved, the thin edge of grass upon gravel having a mean effect. In a long line of flower-beds, rectangles should alternate with circles, tangled thickets of unrelated flowers with masses of the same flower in varied colours, so that there may be the added charm of unity in diversity. The best method of judging minor architectural features, such as piers and stairways, is to consider whether they are bold enough to take their place in a picture.

CHAPTER IV ∴ ∴ ∴ ∴ ∴ ∴ ∴

To make a great garden, one must have a great idea or a great opportunity; a cypress causeway leading to a giant's castle, or a fountain cave where a ceaseless iris plays on a river falling through the roof, or a deep clear pool with an underworld fantasy of dragon-guarded treasure caves lit by unearthly light, or a mighty palace quadrangle lined with hanging gardens of arcaded terraces, or a great galleon in a lake whose decks are dropping with jasmine and myrtle, or a precipitous ravine with double bridges and a terrace on either hand. But it is possible to introduce a touch of imaginative beauty into almost any garden by finding the most perfect form for one of its features, or by giving expression to the soul of some particular flower or tree, as with the Virginian vine on the trellis arcades at Schwetzingen and the cypress in the Giusti avenue at Verona.

So, if it is to be a rose-garden, do not choose those stunted, unnatural, earth-loving strains, which have nothing of vigour and wildness in them, nor banish other flowers which may do homage to the beauty of a rose as courtiers to a queen. Let climbing roses drop in a veil from the terrace and smother with flower-spangled embroidery the garden walls, run riot over vaulted

Cypresses, Palazzo Giusti, Verona

arcades, clamber up lofty obelisks of leaf-tangled trellis, twine themselves round the pillars of a rose-roofed temple, where little avalanches of sweetness shall rustle down at a touch and the dusty gold of the sunshine shall mingle with the summer snow of the flying petals. Let them leap in a great bow or fall in a creamy cataract to a foaming pool of flowers. In the midst of the garden set a statue of Venus with a great bloom trained to her hand, or of Flora, her cornucopia overflowing with white rosettes, or a tiny basin where leaden *amorini* seated upon the margin are fishing with trailing buds. If the place be away from the house and surrounded by forest trees, let there be a rose balloon weighed down by struggling cupids, or the hollow ribs and bellying curves of an old-world ship with ruddy sail and cordage flecked with ivory blossom, or one of those rose-castles which the French romance gave to the garden for a mimic siege in May, low towers of carpenter's work with flanking turrets and iron-studded postern. Such a *Château d'Amour* is represented on many a mediæval casket and mirror-case. Ponderous mangonels are bombarding the fortress with monstrous blossoms, while from the battlements fair ladies hurl down roses still heavy with morning dew full in the faces of the attacking knights [36].

Gardens consecrated to the worship of some

particular flower have been in favour since the
Ancient Sages devoted their old age to the culture
of chrysanthemum or peony, but who has yet
worked out the utmost beauty of blue iris or
silver-chaliced water-lily, of sweet pea or pansy,
or, sacred to the Queen of Heaven, the 'flower and
plant of light'? Who has realised to the full the
glory of vine, or clematis, or honeysuckle, wisteria, or bougainvillea? If it be sculpture that you
seek, try the effect of a fountain court of *amorini*,
where baby loves are climbing the obelisks and
the flower-vases, playing and splashing each other
upon the water-edge, swimming out to a marble
Nef whose mast and sail and homing bows are
festooned with clambering cupids. Turn into marble Watteau's dream, *L'Embarquement pour l'Île de
Cythère* or Fragonard's *Fontaine d'Amour*. Let there be
a children's corner, the Good Shepherd of the Cat-
acombs with a lamb upon His shoulder standing
amongst the little beds, or a Garden of the Happy
Hours, where Time by the sun-dial is fast asleep,
his hands and feet fettered with rose-wreaths,
while on the steps below him the children are
weaving their flower garlands, wrestling, reading,
singing, playing at war and art and marriage. If it
be colour that you desire, let the view from the
low parlour window be a flash of lavender-blue,
centred with gold, remembering that wild Nature's

loveliest effects are in this key of colour, as wit-
ness the hyacinths that repeat the sky, the purple
tide of the heather, the Alpine anemones, the dark-
blue gentians of the Jura pastures; if a wall garden,
throw round it a grey ring of castle walls, for in
art it is only appearances that matter and forgery
is not a crime unless it fails to deceive.[27] Of historic motives for laying out there can never be a
lack. The fruit trees and vine-covered trellises that
tempered the sunshine in the late Roman gardens,
the pergolas and vaulted pavilions of the Normans
in Sicily, the green tunnels of the fourteenth century, the stately arched hedges of Bacon's essay,
are well suited to any country where the summer
heat is oppressive. How interesting to reconstitute
a forgotten type, the garden of Queen Ultrogoth,
the flower-orchard of the Dark Ages, the Paradise
of William the Bad, the Gothic pleasaunce of Cres-
centius, of the *Roman de la Rose*, of Chaucer, of the
King's Quair! In every land there are countless old
houses still disfigured by the bare lawn and tortu-
ous ways of the landscape gardener, and no one
will have lived in vain who is able to restore to one
of them the melodious beauty of which Pope and
Rousseau robbed it.

But we are not forced to confine ourselves to
imaginative reproductions of the past. Invention
was not exhausted in the eighteenth century when

design went out of fashion. I know no reason why we should not have subtly curving terrace fronts and courts that sweep outward like the mouth of a trumpet to enlarge the view, and indeed but for the intrusion of the unhallowed *Giardino Inglese*, this might have been the natural development of the Rococo garden. How many flowery realms there are yet to conquer! Who has yet sought the summer coolness of a water labyrinth with rose-bordered canals, where a great pool serves for a lawn in front of the house and boats may pass among the fruit trees and the flowers; or the quaintness of a garden of autumn fruit, where purple grapes hang in jewelled clusters upon the wall, dwarf pears and fairy apples are touched with quivering gold; where gourds and pump-kins like strange reptiles have crept out of the flower-beds to sun themselves upon the pavers, some great as the wheels of Cinderella's coach, some shaped by nature as punch-bowls or urns or bottles or balloons or writhing serpents, some moulded for sport into dragons' heads and laugh-ing masks and monstrous baroque faces? Who has yet realised the poetry, the forlorn and elfish beauty of a deserted garden? Who has worked out the possibilities of a sea-shore demesne, or of an amphitheatre in a quarried cliff, or – except at Syracuse – of flowery paths that wind their way

across stony abysses? Who has made for himself
the knots and pergolas of a roof terrace where, as
in Seneca's day, orchids may be planted upon the
highest towers and whole forests may shake upon
the tops and turrets of the house? The false perspective which Nero introduced about his Golden
House, giving across the lawns and lakes prospects
of far-off cities, might, if the limitations be frankly
accepted, be developed into a minor art, as indeed
it is in Japan. Flattened curves and contrasts of
foliage are often used to give the illusion of distance, and the method can be carried further, for
with flowering shrubs one may represent a distant
waterfall, or turn a commonplace hill, like that at
Scarborough, into a snow-capped mountain.

But whatever the garden is to be, whether its
roses are to clamber up the eaves of a cottage or the
towers of a palace, this at least is necessary, that it
should be made with a care for the future and a
conviction of the importance of the task. According to Bacon, gardens are for refreshment; not for
pleasure alone, nor even for happiness, but for the
renewing rest that makes labour more fruitful, the
unbending of a bow that it may shoot the stronger.
In the ancient world it was ever the greatest of the
emperors and the wisest of the philosophers that
sought peace and rest in a garden. By the olive
groves and flower-bordered canals of the *Academia*

Plato discussed with his followers the supremacy of reason, the identity of truth and goodness. Among the roses and myrtles and covered walks of the Lyceum Aristotle taught that perfect happiness is to be found in contemplation, in the divine intuitions of reason. Theophrastus left to his pupils the shady theatre of their studies, and amidst the fruit and flowers Epicurus pondered how by wise conduct to attain happiness. In the garden of the Bamboo-Grove Budda taught the conquest of self, and in the Garden of Sorrows a greater teacher was found, for we know that Jesus ofttimes resorted thither with His disciples. The cloistered paradises of Sicily and of the Arabs may have been made for fairer, frailer flowers, but the rose-tangled orchards of the Middle Ages and the great gardens of the Renaissance did not serve for pleasure alone. In the romances we find the company playing chess in the apple-garden, singing, weaving garlands, dancing the carol, looking on at the play of jugglers, tumblers and dancing-girls, but here also they listen to the lay of the troubadour, and here part of the business of government is carried on. In the *Chanson de Roland*, Charlemagne gives audience in a verger to the ambassadors of the Pagan King of Spain, seated on a golden chair of state beside a bush of eglantine under the shadow of a pine tree, and in *Garin le Loherain*, Count Fremont, one of the great barons, receives a messenger sitting in a garden surrounded by his friends. Some of the great pleasure-grounds of the Renaissance were ever crowded with a great retinue of priests and lawyers, architects and painters, doctors and men of letters, to whom they offered change and rest and freedom. Others were the homes of a court, where laws were considered, finance was regulated, envoys were received; where in one arbour the Poet Laureate might be paying his addresses to the Muse, in another the Treasurer be grappling with his budget, while by the fountain under the shadow of the cypresses the Prince and his companions were discussing the doctrines of Plato and the greatness of the ancient world. Many of the letters of René d'Anjou are dated from the garden at Aix, and a century later we find Queen Elizabeth giving audience in her garden at Hampton and one of her courtiers attesting a charter in his *viridarium* at Edzell. The garden, like beauty in landscape, is inimical to all evil passions [37]: it stands for efficiency, for patience in labour, for strength in adversity, for the power to forgive. Perhaps at the last, in contemplation of the recurring miracle of spring and of that eternal stream of life which is ever flowing before our eyes, we may find that it stands for something more – one of the three things the Greek philosopher thought it lawful to pray for, hope to the dying; for along the thread of time and consciousness the individual is never severed from the race; he is but a leaf on a tree, a blossom on a flowering plant; to the ocean of life he goes, and from the ocean he may return again. Gardens have coloured every dream of future life, every hope of happiness in this, and he who can make them more beautiful has helped to exalt the sentiment of religion, poetry, and love. The older descriptions of Paradise are simple renderings of the pleasure-grounds of the Persians and the flower-orchards of the Dark Ages, imagination being able to picture to itself things more perfect than the eye ever saw, but not things diverse in kind [38]. The mind cannot anticipate an unknown sensation; the deaf mute cannot form an idea of sound, nor the man who is blind from birth have a mental vision. Every impression, whatever its elements may be, is an indivisible whole, differing from its parts and even from the sum of them as a chord in music from the notes of which it is composed, or a new flower from the plants that gave it birth [39], and it is thus always in the power of the artist to give us a fresh creation, something different in kind, as different as were the fountain courts of the Renaissance from the gardens of the Arabs, or the terraces of Helmsley from the alleys of Versailles.

St Carlo's unjust judgement on Cardinal Gambara – that the revenues laid out upon his villa would have been better employed in good works – has even now its defenders, and we have yet with us the 'practical man' who, visiting the dream-gardens of Italy, can see nothing in the cypresses but bundles of faggots, in the flower-beds but baskets of vegetables, in the statues and fountains but heaps of road-metal, and goes away sorrowful at heart over the selfishness of these aristocrats, who waste on pride and luxury what might have been given to the poor. Yet in truth such a garden as that of Lante is a world-possession, and the builder of it like a great poet who has influenced the life of thousands, putting them in touch with the greatness of the past, lifting their thoughts and aspirations to a higher level, revealing to them the light of their own soul, opening their eyes to the beauty of the world. Architecture, the most unselfish of arts, belongs to the passer-by, and every old house and garden in which the ideal has been sought is a gift to the nation, to be enjoyed by future generations who will learn from it more of history and art and philosophy than may be found in books. Thus the garden-maker is striving not for himself alone but for those who are to come after, for the unborn children who shall play on the flowery lawns and chase each other through the alleys, filling their laps with treasure of never-fading roses, weaving amidst the flowers and the sunshine

Villa Lante,
Bagnaia

dream-garlands of golden years. They too will share the joys and sorrows of the garden, will learn to love even the humblest tribes of its inhabitants: the prodigal weeds that carry the banners of spring in procession upon the cornices, and the dwarf trees, dead to the world, that have rooted themselves like anchorites in the crevices; the tinted lichen which feed on pure air and sunshine and outlast the stubborn oaks, and the lowly mosses which drink in the dewdrops and the blue shadows of the mighty trees; the sweet-sighing herbs of the twilight; and the pale stars of earth which, stirred from their slumbers when night is dropping dew into the mouths of the thirsty flowers, call the outcast moths to a honeyed banquet. They too will know bare winter's hidden hoard, when the earth under their feet is full of dreams – dim memories of misty morns and dewy eves, of the slumbrous warmth of the golden sunshine, the soft caresses of the life-giving breezes, the nuptial kisses of the bees. They too will feel the rhythmic breath of wakening life from the countless millions of beings in earth and air and dewdrop and rivulet, with the rising murmur of insect delight, the scent of the sun-kissed grasses – all the mystery and music, the riot and rapture of the spring, and the passion of the flaming roses, and that strange thrill of autumn sadness when the flowers that have mingled their perfumes through the summer are breathing out to each other the grief of a last farewell.

It is not given to every man, when his life's work is over, to grow old in a garden he has made, to lose in the ocean roll of the seasons little eddies of pain and sickness and weariness, to watch year after year green surging tides of spring and summer break at his feet in a foam of woodland flowers, and the garden like a faithful retainer growing grey in its master's service. But for him who may live to see it, there shall be a wilder beauty than any he has planned. Nature, like a shy wood-nymph, shall steal softly back on summer nights to the silent domain, shading with tenderest pencillings of brown and grey the ripened stone, scattering wood-violets in the grassy alleys, and wreathing in vine and ivy the trellised arbour, painting with cloudy crusts of crumbly gold the long balustrades, inlaying the cornices with lines of emerald moss, planting little ferns within the fountain basin and tiny patches of green velvet upon the Sea-God's shoulder. As the years pass by and no rude hand disturbs the traces of her presence, Nature becomes more daring. Flower-spangled tapestries of woven tendrils fall from the terrace, strange fleecy mottlings of silver-grey and saffron and orange and greeny-gold make the wall a medley more beautiful than broidered hangings or than painted pictures, the niches are curtained with creepers, the pool is choked with water-plants, blossoming weeds are in every crevice, and with pendent crystals the roof of the grotto is fretted into an Arab vault. Autumn has come at last, and the harvest is being gathered in. Flying shafts of silvery splendour fall upon the fountain, and all the house is dark, save for the strange light that is burning yet in the chamber window. Softly the Triton mourns, as if sobbing below his breath, alone in the moon-enchanted fairyland of a deserted garden.

NOTES TO THE TEXT ∽

1) In 1712, when Addison, stirred by descriptions of travel in China, was proposing to introduce into the garden the 'beautiful wildness of nature,' Watteau was already making it the subject of his pictures. Painting in the great neglected gardens of the Luxembourg and Montmorency, he gives indeed the statues, stairways, and stately hemicycles of the old régime, but the green irregular vistas have no limit, and every trace of regularity in pathway or vegetation has disappeared. In 1717 he produced L'Embarquement pour l'Île de Cythère, 'the first genuine painted poem that Europe had seen since the golden days of the Venetian Renaissance.'

2) So one is told; but the garden is first mentioned in 1644 and appears to have been laid out in the sixteenth century, perhaps by San Michele, who added to or altered the house. The older cypresses, one of which was supposed to be seven hundred years old, belonged to an earlier scheme.

3) The date of the palace and garden is about 1750.

4) The traveller must not miss the charming garden-court of the Palazzo Controni-Pini at Lucca, with its statues and fountains and great red earthen jars set against a background of old grey ramparts, nor that of the Palazzo Giustiniani (Via del Santo, 21) at Padua with its loggia and banqueting house designed by Falconetto; nor those in the Via dei Fiori, Via Moretti, Via Soncino, Via Triest at Brescia. In the town of Como, the Palazzo Giovio, now turned into a museum, has at the end of the garden a terrace commanding a view of the mountain side.

5) I made it 485 paces to the centre of the mound.

6) Via S Lazaro.

7) *Dello Scoglio*. This has colour even on a sunless day.

8) At Villa Muti, Frascati, there is a good combination of slope and stairway. This is all of stone, and following each step is an incline of double the length. The grass steps at Villa Gamberaia have box borders to cover the ragged edges.

9) See the work at Villa d'Este, Tivoli.

10) The largest I have ever seen are at Villa Sormanni, Castelazzo. These are five feet across and about 4 ft. 8 ins. high, made in three portions and held together by iron rings. Smaller pots containing orange trees are lifted into them. In Sicily the mauve flowers of the candytuft are sometimes used to cover the bare earth in the larger flower-vases.

11) Writers on garden-craft assert that the house is the 'one immutable fact' from which everything must start. But those who seek ideal beauty will allow landscape, or landscape and garden in conjunction, to govern the house. It is obvious that where the surrounding scenery offers a quiet background admitting of elaboration in garden design, the house also should be quiet. This does not necessarily mean that it should be plain and unadorned; symmetry and repetition, as at Blickling, will give breadth and repose to a rich façade.

12) The double climax is particularly unpleasant in a wild and picturesque country such as Scotland, and many old Scotch gardens are ruined by it. Intricacy of design seems to be desirable (1) if the garden, being on a very high site or in a plain, is shut in by foliage or castle walls; (2) if a wooded hillside in the middle distance cuts off the distant views; (3) if the middle distance is eliminated by a falling slope, or by lofty hedges, and the distant country is broad and restful. I am unable to agree with Mrs Wharton, whose views however deserve the greatest respect, that the success of the elaborate scheme at Lante is due to the quietness of the distant prospect. I attribute it to the fact that the middle distance is concealed by the hedge and houses immediately

behind the garden, and consider that the town of Bagnaia is a background to the garden, and the far distance a background to the town. At Villa Gamberaia, near Florence, the middle views are lost in the falling ground, and far away are the hillsides beyond the broad Arno valley, sprinkled with white-walled villas which give them scale and modelling and human interest.

13) 'The ideal is a concept formed by the perception of differences and the imaginary prolongation of the direction of such differences to the furthest point within the horizon of apparent possibility. This point, or terminus, is the ideal, but it is far short of the horizon of Nature, which is always transcending it.' W. James, *Principles of Psychology*, i 508.

14) Personification involves the ascription of feelings. L'Evêque (*La Science du beau*, 1872, pp. 93–4) makes a wave of affection for the object part of the emotion of beauty, and I think that in one's own garden there is an illusion of a return wave. The pleasure we derive from colour, scent, and song in the garden is a by-product of evolution, due to that similarity of environment and of the power to respond to it which has cast our senses almost in the same mould with those of the insects and birds; and the significance of the fact is that life is one and man a part of nature, not a supernatural being who has been suddenly intruded into a garden. The discovery that some plants have rudimentary sense-organs, and that the cell nucleus is capable of memory and desire, must revolutionise the whole science of psychology.

15) The object-world of the insects differs strangely from ours. It is a miracle-world in which nothing happens by law, in which the extraordinary freshness of sensation makes sensuous beauty greater, though symbolic beauty be less. Scent is the dominant sense of the insects, enabling them to distinguish not only a greater number of odours, but the

direction, motion, and even the shape of the objects from which such odours spring. Their sight is supposed to be quicker than ours for movement, but less distinct for form. The ultra-violet rays, which with human beings are absorbed by the lens, constitute, as Lubbock points out, for some insects a new and unimaginable colour, differing from violet as green from blue or red from orange, and if these rays enter into the composition of white light and the red are absent, the general aspect of nature cannot be the same. The relative value of colours may also be changed. With our eyes the sensitiveness to green is three hundred and seventy times as great as that for red: with the insects, for all we know, some other colour may be raised to the higher power. Further, it is possible that some insects possessing organs the use of which is unknown may have a sixth sense. Between forty thousand vibrations of the air in a second, giving the highest audible sound, and four hundred million vibrations of the ether, giving the sensation of red, there is room for many unimaginable senses.

16) See the writer's unpublished essay on beauty, in which it is shown that in addition to the recognised elements of aesthetic pleasure, there are in the mind natural sympathies of power, freedom, happiness, and reason, and emotions or passions of ideality and personality.

17) It is to these harmonies that Michelangelo must have been referring when he spoke of spoiling his music. Many things which do not come within the field of our ordinary consciousness are recorded in the lower conscious centres. See Forel, *The Senses of Insects*, p. 298.

18) The sublime is an emotion raised by overwhelming power or magnitude or duration of time; that is to say, overwhelming in comparison with our own significance. There is thus sublimity of power, freedom, height, strength, vastness, and duration, which may or may not be mixed with

beauty. In the presence of the sublime, the consciousness of self is lost (Spencer, i 231 ii 438 pars 98, 439), and all irrelevant and trivial ideas are excluded.

19) The softness of turf gives a light heart, and sounds which repeat themselves, such as the bubbling of a fountain, the cawing of rooks, the song of the cuckoo, strike a note of peacefulness. The total impression of a garden is built up not only of sensation interpreted by perception, but also of sentiment and emotion, and the interest of the house, the beauty of the landscape as seen from the garden, the character and historical associations of the surrounding country, even the circumstances under which one first visited the place, have a share in shaping it. Such an impression is an indivisible whole and the sentiment attached to it makes it distinctive as a chord in music.

20) In addition to the pleasure of sensation, there is a vague and baffling suggestion of other delights. This is probably due to re-representation below the threshold of the joys which other gardens have given. As with wild animals a certain scent will render nascent in idea the motor changes which accompany the running down, seizing, killing, and eating of the prey, so in this case the memory of other experiences is stirred, but so faintly that it eludes our grasp, like a name we cannot quite recall. Sometimes the actual scene may be reproduced. Compare Spencer's *Psychology*, 1870, i 61, 191, 308, 484; ii 638 (pars 22, 76, 140, 214, 536). There seems also to be a suggestion of flavour, the very message the flowers are sending to the bees and indeed smell must be considered as taste at a distance, just as sight is distant touch. Grant Allen points to the dwindled olfactory lobes as proof that smell is an atrophied sense which has outlived its principal uses, and considers that it now yields relatively large emotional waves and relatively small intellectual information; in fact, that it has sunk

into a sentimental old age. Many flowers which are wind fertilised exhale perfume, and according to Maeterlinck the original function of perfumes is unknown. I venture to suggest that it was to lessen evaporation, scented air being opaque to the heat rays. If perfumes are to be described by poets or scientists, new terms must be invented; in the rose alone seventeen different varieties of scent have been distinguished by experts, and to find a proper epithet for the odour of the box leaf we should have to combine the adjectives warm, sweet, bitter, clean, aromatic.

21) Spencer's *Psychology*, i 492, ii 594, 641 (pars 216, 519, 537). In this revival of other associated feelings of pleasure, it must be presumed that the senses of hearing and smell play an important part, these having greater power to gather round them accretions of mood and sentiment, though impressions of sight are more easily reproduced in memory. Every one has noticed the feeling roused by the cawing of rooks, the perfume of new-mown hay, the voice of an old friend heard unexpectedly.

22) I think that instinct in animals will some day be explained as inherited memory in the form of an idea; that is to say, an inherited tendency for a certain tract in the brain to react to a particular stimulus. Spencer draws practically no distinction between memory, idea, and desire (*Psychology*, par 213).

23) Those things are real which are judged by our senses to belong, like the body, to the world of space; that is to say, not to the world of things as they are, but to the world of things as they feel.

24) At Vicenza.

25) The bust on the pulpit, formerly supposed to be a portrait of Sigelgaita the wife of the donor, is now held to be a representation of the city of Ravello. In classic times, cities

were often represented by ideal figures, and the practice was revived in the thirteenth and again in the fifteenth century. Il Tribolo placed a bronze statue of a woman, representing the City of Florence, upon his fountain at Castello. At Villa Garzoni there are seventeenth-century statues of Lucca and Florence.

26) James *Psychology*, ii 173–4, 89. The eye cannot avoid following the movement of a waterfall, but continually recovers its position by a series of jerks. Exner has shown that the sensation of motion is distinct from that of colour in the human eye, where it has a special place in the lateral periphery of the retinal field, completely independent of the perception of objects. The faceted eyes of insects are specially adapted for the detection of movement. See Auguste Forel, *The Senses of Insects*, 1908, p. 8.

27) Near Pallanza on Lake Maggiore there is a strangely successful castle ruin built to protect a private garden from being overlooked from the windows of an hotel near by.

REFERENCES IN THE TEXT ⌐⌐

[1] 'A New Voyage to Italy,' ii 65, 291.

[2] G S Hillard, Six Months in Italy, 1853.

[3] Modern Painters, 1898, v 218 (part ix chap i par iv).

[4] Forel, The Senses of Insects, 1908, 3 122 196; Lubbock, The Senses of Animals 1889, 191–3.

[5] W James, Principles of Psychology, 1891, ii 298.

[6] Modern Painters, 1898, iii 140–1 (part iv chap x pars 8–9) 298–301 (part iv chap xvii pars 3–7).

[7] Ferrier, The Functions of the Brain, 1876, 257–9.

[8] Spencer, Principles of Psychology, 1870, i 178 477 485 562 565–6 (pars 71 211 214 245 246); James, Psychology, 1891, i 562.

[9] Modern Painters, 1898, iii 297–9 (iii xvii pars 2 3 4); James, Psychology, i 558–9 254–5.

[10] James, Psychology, i 479 note.

[11] Spencer, Psychology, i 485 493–4 571 (pars 214 216 247).

[12] Spencer, Psychology, 1870, i 191 258 (pars 76 116).

[13] Spencer, Psychology, i 599–601; ii 593–4 (pars 261 519).

[14] Spencer, Psychology, ii 295.

[15] Spencer, Psychology, 1870, i 466 491 570; ii 580 (pars 208 216 247 514).

[16] James, Psychology, ii 428.

[17] Spencer, Psychology, 1870, i 485 (par 214).

[18] Modern Painters, ii 45–7 (part iii sec i chap v pars 6–8).

[19] Modern Painters, 1897, i xl.

[20] Modern Painters, 1898, iii 310 (part iv chap xvii par 22).

[21] Modern Painters, 1897, ii 34 (part iii sec i chap iv par 4).

[22] James, Psychology, i 575.

[23] James, Psychology, ii 316; Grant Allen, Physiological Aesthetics, 1877, 175–80.

[24] Ruskin, Seven Lamps of Architecture, chap v.

[25] Spencer, Psychology, par 539.

[26] See Sir Joshua Reynolds' Fourteenth Discourse.

[27] Raymond, Essentials of Aesthetics, 1907, 153–4; Ruskin, Modern Painters, 1898, iii 141–8 (part iv chap x pars 9–18); James, Psychology, 1891, ii 124.

[28] Bain, Rhetoric, 1892, ii 29 53 206.

[29] Ruskin, Stones of Venice, vol iii chap i par 7.

[30] Turner's Harbours of England, 1856; note on the drawing of Scarborough.

[31] Modern Painters 1897, i 345–55 (part ii sec v chap i pars 1–10).

[32] James, Psychology, ii 81.

[33] Modern Painters, 1900, i 380 (part ii sec v chap iii par 8).

[34] Sir Montagu Pollock, Light and Water.

[35] Sir Montagu Pollock, Light and Water, 1903, 61 note.

[36] J Westwood, Description of the Fictile Ivories of the South Kensington Museum, 1883, 297 299 300 309.

[37] Ruskin, Modern Painters iii 308 312 (part iv chap xvii pars 18 26–30).

[38] Spencer, Psychology, par 187; James, Psychology, ii 44; Ruskin, Modern Painters iii ii ii 10 and iv iii 23.

[39] James, Psychology i 488 ii 2 note 30 45 270; Spencer, Psychology, par 211.

INDEX ∽

A NOTE ON THE TYPE ∽

ON THE MAKING OF GARDENS has been set in a digital version of Monotype Joanna, a type designed by Eric Gill for use at Hague & Gill, the private press he operated with his son-in-law, René Hague. Like Gill's best-known type, Perpetua, the letterforms of Joanna are clearly descendants of Gill's inscriptional lettering rather than conventional calligraphic or typographic models. In its proportions and close letter-fitting, the present type bears a strong family resemblance to both Perpetua and Golden Gockerel, one of Gill's most striking (if least known) types. Joanna's distinctive appearance, due in large part to near-monoline strokes and slab serifs, seems to stand as a challenge to designers, who commonly — and unfairly — relegate it to use as a display type. Yet Joanna's strong vertical emphasis and singularly narrow italic make it an elegant text face, one that serves happily in small volumes with unjustified text blocks, as can be seen in Gill's own Essay on Typography (1931), one of the first books to be set in Joanna.

Design and composition by Carl W. Scarbrough